HERE YOU ARE, COURAGEOUS

TRANSFORM YOUR RELATIONSHIP WITH FEAR, ANXIETY AND PANIC AND RECLAIM YOUR LIFE

LAUREN ROSE

Published in the United States by: Hay House LLC: www.hayhouse.com®
Published in Australia by: Hay House Australia Publishing Pty Ltd: www.hayhouse.com.au
Published in the United Kingdom by: Hay House UK Ltd: www.hayhouse.co.uk
Published in India by: Hay House Publishers (India) Pvt Ltd: www.hayhouse.co.in

Cover design: Rhett Nacson
Typeset by: Bookhouse, Sydney
Edited by Margie Tubbs
Author Photo by Lisa Ray

Cataloging-in-Publication Data is on file at the Library of Congress

Tradepaper ISBN: 9781401994419
E-book ISBN: 9781401996284

10 9 8 7 6 5 4 3 2 1
1st edition, 2024

For Lila
&
Juliet

CONTENTS

INTRODUCTION

– This book began its life as a very different story to the one you now have before you.

When I first set out to write it – over ten years ago now – I had every intention of writing an honest and definitive guide on how to overcome an anxiety disorder. Newly diagnosed, and heavily afflicted with recurrent panic attacks, I'd taken to reading every book on panic and anxiety that I could get my hands on. Frustratingly, I found them either too clinical and complicated, laden with medical terminology and lengthy techniques that didn't seem to translate into the real world, or the opposite: written as if they were aimed at a young child, with cartoon diagrams and acronyms that made me cringe. What I wanted was a book that would tell me explicitly how to get through the day when it felt like my body was on fire. I wanted to read about the things I was experiencing in a way that sounded like the author had actually experienced them too.

There's a quote by famous children's author Beverly Cleary that goes, '*If you don't see the book you want on the shelf, write it.*[1] So that's what I had decided to do. With a catchy title in mind, and a chapter outline at the ready, I envisioned a book that would accompany the reader as they battled their way through their fears; finally coming out the other side victorious, free from anxiety and panic and excited to reclaim their life. If there was a part of me that thought it might be questionable to write a book about overcoming anxiety when I hadn't yet managed to overcome it myself, it was silenced by the desire to write something – anything – that would help.

I couldn't have known back then the gravity of the journey I was about to embark upon. What I thought was going to be a process of ridding myself of anxiety, and then writing about it in a way that was honest and (hopefully) helpful, ended up being a total rebuilding of my relationship with fear. What I imagined would look like a re-invention of self; a triumphant and sparkly debut featuring the new and improved me (far less afraid, and preferably liberated from digestive disturbances, too) turned out to be more of a *return* to self. A deep and grateful acknowledgement of who and *how* I am: afraid, digestively disturbed and otherwise. In consuming every bit of information I could find on my disorder, anticipating that the more knowledge I had about anxiety, the better equipped I'd be at divorcing myself from it, I wound up uncovering a vast sense of fascination and awe, not just for my disorder, but for me, and the beautiful ways in which those two forces collide. I knew the pathway to healing wouldn't be linear, but I didn't expect it to come right back around to the exact place I'd started from.

So, although this isn't the book that I intended on writing all those years ago, I hope that it is better than that book could ever have been. Within these pages, you will find a sincere exploration of the landscape of anxiety: from the biology of the anxiety response and the continuous dance between internal systems, to the anguish and heartache that comes alongside a body doused in fear. We will discuss the nature of the subconscious and the propensity to the familiar, and the urge to run, to repress, to resist, even when we know it's not in our best interest to do so.

But, more than that – we will talk about adventure. We will dive into connection, community, and courage. We will seek pleasure, we will discover purpose, we will unfurl into inhabiting our bodies again. Because these are equally important parts of the conversation. We cannot talk about anxiety without also talking about the humans who experience it. We cannot talk about fear without talking about courage, too.

▪

I know that it hasn't been easy. You've fought, you've pushed, you've persisted. And still, you are here, and that is no small feat. I also want you to know that this space where you find yourself; this gap between fighting and giving in, this is *exactly* where you are supposed to be. This strange, messy middle: this is the place where you will discover who you are, what you want, and what it is you are here to do. We are going to take a journey together, you and I, and this journey is not one of becoming fearless, or of learning how to mute the anxiety enough to 'get by'.

This is a pathway home to your truest nature.

So get yourself cosy, find a soft nest to sit in, take a deep breath and let the adventure begin.

PART ONE
FEAR

CHAPTER 1
DIAGNOSIS

It feels like I'm dying.

– At twenty-three years old, it seemed like a dramatic statement to make. Especially given that I knew I wasn't *actually* dying: the barrage of medical tests I'd requested had all shown that I was physically in perfect health. I didn't know how else to put it, though. How to summarise what I was experiencing in a way that that my doctor would really understand. Because in a span of just over twelve months, I had gone from being a busy young woman with two part time jobs and an active social life to being too afraid to leave my house, most days. I had quit working, I had stopped seeing friends. I had begun avoiding anything that required me to sit in a car, or stand in a queue, or be more than a few metres away from a bathroom. I may not have been dying, but it sure didn't feel like I was living, either.

It had started on what was otherwise an unremarkable morning. I'd just clocked on for my usual shift as a sales assistant at a small stationary store, and somewhere between the cash register and the greeting card aisle, I was hit with a sudden wave of nausea. I paused, and stood up straight. A chill prickled across my skin: I was cold, then hot, then cold again. I could hear a sort of static buzz reverberating in my ear drums – it was overwhelmingly noisy, like the volume had been turned up on everything all at once. Excusing myself, I rushed to the bathroom and took long, deep breaths, gripping the porcelain edges of the basin to try and steady myself. As I stared at my reflection in the grimy mirror above the sink, I saw the colour visibly draining from my skin. I wondered if I was about to faint. I'd never fainted before, but I was certain it must feel something like this.

I took myself home shortly after; heading straight to bed to sleep off whatever virus I assumed I was coming down with. After a few hours, though, I felt completely fine, so by the time the next morning rolled around, I was back at work ready to pick up where I'd left off the day before.

Until the same thing happened again. I'd no sooner put my handbag away and walked out onto the sales floor when another wave of nausea hit. Only this time, it was laced with a kind of urgency that knocked the air out of my lungs, and I felt sweaty and scared and desperate to get away, but with no idea what I was trying to get away from. Once again, I rushed to the bathroom and leaned over the wash basin, sucking in air while repeating over and over in my head *You're okay. You're okay. You're okay.*

I didn't leave work early that day, partly because I didn't think I could get away with it for a second day in a row without seriously pissing off my boss, but also because there was something about the way that I felt that made me not want to draw attention to it. I spent the remainder of the shift trying to appear normal while my hands shook and my stomach churned and my breath caught in my throat. Each time I had to make another mad dash to the toilet, I would pretend like it was because I was drinking so much water: I *need to pee, again, can you believe it?*, instead of explaining the honest truth, which was that I was having repetitive bouts of diarrhoea. I'd smile and act casual while walking to the bathroom, and then I'd lock the cubicle door and hang my head in my hands, trembling and wondering what the f**k was happening to me, and what could I do to make it go away?

And that was how it continued. For more than a year, I shrank further into myself as my body became host to a range of inexplicable, relentless sensations that I couldn't predict or control; symptoms of a mystery illness that never seemed to ease.

Stomach cramps, nausea, loose and urgent bowel movements. Dizzy spells, breathlessness, numbness in my hands and feet. When listed out individually, the symptoms didn't seem so bad. I knew this, because each time I sat in front of a health professional and mumbled them under my breath, ashamed and embarrassed, none of them so much as flinched.

They'd all nodded their heads and scribbled down notes, and offered the occasional reassuring smile – but not one of them had looked at me and said, *'oh'*, as if they got it. As if they knew. Because it wasn't so much the symptoms themselves as the space they took up in my body and mind. To say that I was uncomfortable *all of the time* seemed almost a ridiculous understatement. It was so much more than that. I was exhausted; tired of clenching my teeth and trying to hold myself together, in the most literal sense. Also, I was afraid, and I couldn't quite figure out why. Perhaps it was because no one seemed to be able to tell me what was going on with me. Perhaps it was because I only seemed to be getting worse. I genuinely felt unwell, like my body was falling apart from the inside out. Yet test after test had showed that there was nothing wrong; nothing was out of place, nothing was enlarged or inflamed or otherwise accountable for the assortment of pain and discomfort I was experiencing. It was almost like I was going crazy – imagining an internal destruction that wasn't really happening at all.

Still, every time my gut churned, every time my skin prickled and my heart thudded in my chest and the hairs on the back of my neck stood up ... all of it felt so incredibly *loud* within me, it just didn't seem possible that there was no medical explanation.

Until finally, I received a diagnosis.

You are suffering from agoraphobia, anxiety, and depression, my doctor told me. He wrote the words down on a piece of paper, underlining each one as if to drive the point home. I remember putting a mental question mark next to agoraphobia – I had no idea what that term even meant.

He went on to assure me that with the right medication (antidepressants to help correct the 'chemical imbalance' in my brain, and antipsychotics to help me 'get some rest') along with a referral for cognitive behavioural therapy, I would be back to normal in no time at all. *Don't worry*, he said. *Okay?*

Of course, I did worry.

The whole car ride home from the doctor's office, I sobbed. I didn't understand where all of this – this depression, anxiety, and agoraphobia (whatever that was) – had come from. Things in my life had been great. I'd been happy before my body had started spontaneously exploding on me. In fact, I'd worked really, really hard at getting myself to a good place, mentally speaking. It wasn't the first time I'd been diagnosed with a chemical imbalance. As a teenager, I had experienced bouts of depression, self-harm and suicide attempts, and had been prescribed antidepressant medication to correct my – allegedly – imbalanced brain a number of times. And yet, I couldn't help feeling like this wasn't the same thing. I knew what depression felt like: I'd been to those blunt-edged places in my mind before and this seemed so different. Where depression had felt numb, dark and empty, this felt almost electric. It was as if my entire body was connected to a live-wire, and someone kept turning the dial up to full charge. I could feel *everything*, in the most agonising way. I was desperate for it to stop.

The night that I received my diagnosis, I went and did what any self-respecting millennial would do: I googled. A lot. I discovered that the strange 'attacks' I'd been experiencing

– the ones where my body felt as if it were exploding – were panic attacks: a physical manifestation of fear and anxiety, so intense and extreme that they often lead sufferers to believe that they are dying. I learned about panic disorder, a condition characterised by recurring panic attacks, which can often develop into *agoraphobia*: excessive fear of being in situations and/or places from which escape may be difficult, coupled with the need to avoid such situations and/or places. I found out that, far from being a completely random anomaly (or the result of an 'imbalanced' mind – more on this in chapter 3) anxiety disorders affect an estimated 301 million people worldwide[2], with women being nearly twice as likely than men to experience some kind of anxiety disorder in their lifetime.

For the most part, I was relieved. I now had a name for what was happening to me; a way to neatly pack and label this mess I'd found myself in, which meant that I'd hopefully have a way to remove it, too. The medical websites echoed my doctor's sentiments—cognitive behavioural therapy and medication were listed as the recommended treatment for anxiety disorders, and the outcomes appeared to be positive (the words 'treatable' and 'manageable' featured repeatedly).

I was also heartened by the confirmation that I hadn't been imagining it after all. This was a real, medically diagnosed illness, not an overreaction or something I'd simply dreamt up. This disorder had attached itself to me through no fault of my own, and now I just had to do the work of untangling myself from the panic and the fear, and I'd find my way back to the life that I'd worked so hard at creating.

There was a tiny part of me, though, that wondered if it was really going to be that straightforward. Because nestled amongst the medical websites and the articles written by someone who obviously had some distance from these disorders, there was post after post (after post) from those who were suffering with panic and anxiety and hadn't yet found their way out. There was even a series of comments in which people compared the years agoraphobia had 'stolen' from them: *I've been housebound for nearly a decade! Versus I managed to recover after five years, but then I relapsed and now I'm back at square one.* The more I read, the more I began to notice a huge disparity between the outcomes predicted by the medical websites, and the reality of those who were living through it.

That's not going to be me, I vowed. *I will beat this. I will find a way through.*

It was less than twelve hours later that those intentions were seriously challenged. Determined to prove that I could overpower my panic, I'd asked my mum to drive me to a local shopping centre. I'd managed to keep my head down for most of the journey, sitting in the passenger seat with my feet up on the dashboard, distracting myself by keeping my eyes on my phone screen. We were almost there when I made the mistake of looking up at the road ahead, and that's when every cell in my body started to turn on me. It happened simultaneously; the stomach ache, the tingling hands, the fear creeping up and down the back of my neck. It was like my entire being was folding in on itself – it was too much and not anywhere near enough, all at the same time. *Turn around*, I'd shrieked. *I can't do this.* And I couldn't. I really couldn't take one more second of sitting in that car.

There's a certain kind of dread that comes alongside a panic attack when you're away from your 'safe place'. It's a desperate need to be back in your familiar environment *immediately*, combined with the knowledge that you still have a ways to go to get there … and the result is absolutely crushing. In those moments, there is simply nowhere to go – no way of escaping yourself, no way of stopping or soothing the terror in your body and mind.

And, when given the choice – wouldn't you choose to avoid that terror? Wouldn't you choose to stay safe and calm over the possibility of feeling scared to death?

Physically, I chose safety. I became obsessed with the belief that there had to be way to overcome my anxiety that didn't involve putting myself in the eye of the storm. I spent hours online, researching agoraphobia and panic; using every possible search term I could think of to come up with a different result. There had to be some type of medication, or cutting-edge therapy, or some kind of down-loadable click funnel program that would cure me of these disorders. Someone out there knew how to beat this fear, and if I had to pay four monthly payments of $399 in order to find them, then dammit, I was stuffed, because I did *not* have that kind of money.

I was still taking my medication and attending therapy (on the days I could manage it, at least) but I wasn't getting any better. If anything, it was becoming even harder to get out of bed in the morning and face the day. I felt defeated.

I didn't understand what I was doing wrong. I raged at how difficult it was; how impossible and stupid that the one thing that was supposed to help me (leaving the house) was the one thing I couldn't do. If I could just eliminate these feelings in my body – if I could somehow find a way to turn off the anxiety that charged through me every second of the day, then I would be alright. *Then* I could start to focus on healing.

But how do you heal a body that you can't control? How do you fix a mind that won't listen to reason? How do you fight your fears, when your fears are fighting you?

CHAPTER 2

YOU ARE NOT BROKEN

Being human is a courageous act.
- Rebecca Campbell, *The Rose Oracle*

– What I wish had happened when I sat in that doctors office, telling him that it felt like I was dying, is this: I wish that he had taken my hands in his, looked me in the eyes and said:

Sometimes, I feel that way too. Sometimes, to be human is to be scared. To feel overwhelmed. To feel like your fear is going to suffocate you. But there are ways in which you can get to know fear; fear is not an enemy of courage, but an ally. Right now it may feel like your body is working against you, and that you are drowning in trying to hold on. But, together, we can turn towards the body. We can learn the language of the body – it speaks in sensation and feelings, not in words. We can soften our grip on control, we can learn to not cling so tightly to resistance. You can and you will grow through this. Your anxiety is not something that we need to fix or cure;

your humanness is your birthright. The more time we spend sitting here trying to find a way to eliminate and remove your anxiety, the more time you will spend feeling anxious.

If you approach your fear and worry as abnormal – as if it is some error to be fixed – it is here that you will end up fragmented. Fragmented into the 'you' that is wrong, sick and broken ... and the 'you' that is trying to avoid the wrong, sick and broken parts.

Instead, it took me years to learn those lessons. It took me days and weeks and months of avoidance, of pain, of tears and torment before I really understood that everything I thought was 'wrong' with me was not what was wrong with me at all.

This is not where I launch into a spiel about anxiety being your superpower, by the way. I know that when you've spent hours wanting to tear your own skin off because you're crawling with discomfort, you don't want a superpower, you just want to be able to peacefully exist. And I get that ... believe me, I do.

But this is where I tell you that you are not, and never have been broken. That there is no part of you or your anxiety that needs to be managed or treated or cured. You are not broken – you are human, and the innate need to survive is one of the most human feelings there is.

Every time we try to separate ourselves from the complexity of our own human nature, we lose sight of who we really are. We forget that we are thinking, feeling creatures, expressive and emotive, bursting with conflicting desires and needs. We are chaotic and curious, we are tender and real. Our experience on this earth is supposed to reflect that, if we are truly willing to be honest with ourselves. Although I understand the urge to part with the messiness of it all – because, certainly, it would be easier to do so – we would be forfeiting everything that ultimately makes us feel alive.

If only we gave ourselves the grace to explore what is really within each of us – the resilience, the creativity, the compassion, the honest vulnerability and tremendous strength – we would see that the things we think are so wrong with us are the things that allow us to connect, achieve and live wholeheartedly. I'm not saying that it's our perceived 'shortcomings' that make us special, but it is the presence of our limitations as well as our virtues that makes us whole. It is both. It was always both.

Sometimes, to be human is to be scared. To feel over-whelmed. To feel like your fear is going to suffocate you.

And so, I know.

I know how jarring it is to feel as if you've been split down the middle. As if there is the you from *before*: the one who used to laugh and say yes to life, the one who knew how to play and create and live, unhindered by constraints and the ceaseless fear of 'what if'. And then there is you of *now* – the one who can't seem to eat or sleep properly, the one who never feels safe, never feels held, never feels fully rested because every single moment is consumed by fear and worry and dread.

I know how frustrating it is to try to explain to a medical professional that where you once had a life, you now just have a series of hours that are passing you by. To tell them how it feels like your body is your enemy; that its sensations are killing you … only to be given a medication that promises more sensations as a side effect.

I know how absolutely infuriating it can be to search desperately for answers, and not find a single one that tells you exactly how to fix yourself.

But maybe we've been asking the wrong question all along.

Maybe, it's not that we were broken, but that we didn't know what it meant to be whole.

CHAPTER 3
DISORDER

⚊

I panic at a lot of other places besides the disco.
- Author unknown

– The word 'anxiety' has many connotations, depending on who you're talking to. For some, anxiety is a low-level unease that foreshadows something nerve-wracking, like a speech or a job interview. For others, it is all-consuming – a full-body force of dread, less of a shadow and more of an overwhelming darkness, an unrelenting monster that chews you up and spits you out, over and over again.

At its core, anxiety is a normal physical and psychological response to an unknown or imagined threat, designed to aid in our survival as a species. If we perceive a potential threat to our wellbeing, either consciously or unconsciously, anxiety is the feeling that follows. It is that strange and unsettling heightening of our senses, a personal alarm system to enable us to identify and avoid possible danger.

In the case of anxiety disorders, however, the anxiety response becomes maladaptive; that is, it harms more than it helps. The feeling of anxiety is present more than it logically should be, or is extreme, out of context or grossly disproportionate to the situation. Anxiety disorders are the name we give to an anxiety response that doesn't quite turn off – when people, places and things that should feel comfortable suddenly feel impossible to bear. When you are living in a body that is perpetually uneasy, any sense of wellbeing is quickly eradicated. Of course, this is when the anxiety response itself becomes the threat. We are anxious because we are anxious, we panic because we panic and, like a snake eating its own tail, it becomes hard to know where one ends and where the other begins.

The categories of anxiety disorders and their corresponding definitions are as similar as they are unique. For example, for someone with obsessive-compulsive disorder (OCD), the compulsion to say a certain phrase to a loved one before they leave the house is matched by an overwhelming fear of what might happen to that loved one if they don't say that phrase. Similarly, someone with post-traumatic stress disorder (PTSD) may experience intrusive thoughts, flashbacks and recurring nightmares relating to a traumatic event, matched by an unbearable need to avoid anything that may remind them of that traumatic event. And for those with agoraphobia (hello!), the desperation to be able to escape easily is matched by the intense need to create a safe zone that is as small and controlled as possible. The overarching theme in all of the above cases is fear, and the way in which we cope with (or otherwise avoid) that fear.

This became very clear to me when I started my podcast, *Us Anxious Folk*. As I interviewed people from all over the world experiencing various indications of anxiety, I noticed that although the labels we have been given (or bestow upon ourselves) are different, the underlying fears are generally the same. We fear being unable to cope, whether that's being humiliated in a social setting, having a bowel or urinary accident in public, becoming very ill or close to death (or dying), something unimaginably terrible happening to a loved one, or something unimaginably terrible happening to us. And regardless of the cause of the fear or the way in which we categorise it, the sensation of the fear is the same. This is because the fear response is the same for all of us.

When the fear response kicks in, the sensations felt in the body are immediate. Racing heartbeat, shortness of breath – that 'dropping' feeling in the pit of your stomach. The way your vision seems to blur around the edges, and the world seems just that little bit too bright. Sounds become unbearably loud yet distant and tinny, hands and feet tingle, your skin dampens with perspiration and the tiny little hairs on your arms stand up. And when the fear response kicks in again and again and again before you've even sat down to eat breakfast, the effects on your mental and emotional state feel even worse than the physical sensations.

For example, there's that inescapable sense of something being wrong with you. The need to say 'no' to everything. Feeling like a failure. Forever working yourself into a state, sick with worry over something that would otherwise seem trivial, like a coffee date, a phone call or a trip to the supermarket to pick up milk. Constant obsession with what others might be thinking of you; replaying conversations over and over to pick at all the stupid things you said. Being unable to commit. Being unable to wear restrictive clothing. Being unable to escape the disappointment you feel with the way your life has turned out – the time you've wasted, the things you've missed out on, the ways in which you've abandoned yourself. The fear of feeling this way forever. The fear of what you'll have to do, in order not to feel this way forever.

It's a lot, so it's no wonder we wind up getting anxious about the way that we feel.

But, let's zoom back in on that anxiety for a moment.

I want to talk about what's really going on in our bodies and brains when we feel anxious, because a large part of what adds fuel to the anxious fire is that sense that what's happening to us is somehow 'wrong'. Actually, everything that seems strange and inexplicable about anxiety, biologically speaking, has a clear and specific cause (though I will admit that knowing this doesn't change it, but it does put us in a position to be able to offer compassion towards ourselves when experiencing it).

There are two key areas of your brain that I want to talk about in relation to your felt experience of anxiety: the limbic system and the prefrontal cortex. The limbic system is the oldest and most primitive part of your brain – this is where your internal alarm system starts up. The limbic system is also the area that deals with emotions, memories and arousal, which is why it's sometimes referred to as the 'emotional brain'. The prefrontal cortex is the newer, shinier part of the brain; it's the area responsible for planning, rational thought, social behaviour moderation and emotional regulation, among other things. It doesn't fully develop until well after adolescence. This is why a toddler is the least rational person you will ever meet.

Located within the limbic system is the amygdala, an almond-shaped cluster of nuclei responsible for autonomic emotional responses, such as fear, anxiety, pleasure and so on. It's also responsible for deciding where memories are stored in the brain, and attaching emotional significance to these memories. For example, what you ate for lunch yesterday probably has far less emotional significance than the first time you experienced a panic attack. The amygdala places that panic attack memory in a location where it can be very easily brought to mind, whereas the memory of what you ate for lunch gets assigned to the murky depths of your brain, where all the other unimportant and unmemorable information goes.

Your brain is constantly processing information. When a possible threat is detected among that information, the thalamus – a little area at the top of the brainstem which processes external stimuli and directs it to the relevant areas of the brain – sends a signal to both the prefrontal cortex and the amygdala. The amygdala immediately jumps on this information of 'potential threat' and triggers the sympathetic nervous system to go into action. This is also known as your 'fight or flight response'.

What happens next is that you will physically start to 'feel' the anxiety in your body. Your adrenal glands release a flood of hormones into the bloodstream, including cortisol (stress hormone), adrenaline and noradrenaline. The purpose of this cascade of hormones is to cause rapid physiological changes that help prepare the body to either stay to fight the threat, or run away to safety ('fight' and 'flight', respectively). These physiological changes include an increase in blood pressure and heart rate, dilation of pupils, redirection of blood flow, and an increase in perspiration and muscle tension – including the contraction of inner anal and bladder sphincters, and the temporary pause of any non-essential bodily systems – such as the digestive and immune systems.

This process is involuntary and largely unconscious, occurring in the space of milliseconds. By the time you are feeling the physical effects of these changes, the fight or flight response is already well underway.

But let's go back and revisit the thalamus for a minute. Remember that the thalamus also sent this information to the prefrontal cortex – the rational, thinking part of the brain. The message of 'potential threat' takes longer to hit the prefrontal cortex than the amygdala. The reason for this is because the pathway to the prefrontal cortex from the thalamus is literally longer than the pathway from the thalamus to the amygdala. In other words, the amygdala received the information faster because of its close proximity to the thalamus. This is by design … you need to be able to act quickly in a situation of life or death.

Once the prefrontal cortex (finally) receives the message, it's able to assess the threat and decide whether or not the threat is real and worthy of your reaction. It's then able to communicate back to the amygdala to ramp up the stress response – in the event that it truly is a life-or-death situation, via a further release of cortisol, or whether to calm down via arousal of the parasympathetic nervous system, also known as the 'rest and digest' response.

When the parasympathetic nervous system kicks in, what occurs is more or less the 'undoing' of all of the changes triggered by the sympathetic nervous system. For example, heart rate decreases, pupils constrict, breathing slows down, digestive and immune systems are stimulated to resume function, and internal bladder and anal sphincters relax.

The prefrontal cortex is very much like the responsible adult of your brain, assessing the situation and calmly deciding what level of response is appropriate and necessary, then telling the amygdala what course of action to take. It bears repeating though, this is after the amygdala has already reacted in its primal, survival-focused, instinctual way. You don't burn your hand on a hot flame and consider how much it hurts while your hand is still in the flame, you whip your hand away as quickly as possible and only then do you consider the pain. The survival instinct is a reflex reaction, before conscious thought.

So for those of us with anxiety disorders, why does our prefrontal cortex not kick in and stimulate the parasympathetic nervous system, once we realise that our survival isn't at stake? One study suggests that the prefrontal cortex gets weakened over time from too much stress, so its ability to regulate the anxiety response weakens[3]. Another school of thought suggests that the amygdala shuts out the prefrontal cortex, much like a cranky teenager who slams the door shut on their parents to avoid another lecture.

To me, it makes sense that if the anxiety response itself has become the threat – the physiological changes such as a racing heart, dry mouth and blurred vision causing us to wonder *what the f**k is wrong with me?* – then the presence of this threat is going to continue arousing the sympathetic nervous system, causing an increase in the very sensations we're trying to escape. It's the chemical version of running on a hamster wheel; cortisol is repeatedly being released, as a reaction to it being released in the first place. This is where, I believe, the idea of 'disorder' really comes into play. It's not so much that the body is wrong or even malfunctioning, but that the natural order of our necessary systems has become disrupted. It is not in the removal of any one system that we rediscover balance and inner harmony, it is by love and attention to all systems.

In Chapter 1, I spoke about my experiences of repeatedly being diagnosed with a chemical imbalance. From the moment this was presented to me in my mid-teens (along with a script for medication to 'correct' it), I felt myself internally rallying against it. I was seventeen years old and experiencing my first real heartbreak, but I was assured that the culprit for my intense emotions was not so much the highs and lows of teenage love (and the hit to a very fragile ego), but instead the uneven levels of serotonin in my brain.

I still have the journal entry I wrote from that initial week on medication, where I described not being able to connect to any emotion at all. I was not happy, not sad, but numb … floating above myself in a strange, disassociated sort of way. Over the course of my late teens and early twenties, the chemical imbalance refrain was repeated to me again and again, yet I could never see myself in it. And then, after years of questioning it, the chemical imbalance theory was finally disproved.

In 2022, an umbrella study by University College London[4] found that there was never any scientific evidence to show a relationship between serotonin deficiency and depression, and the whole chemical imbalance argument was turned on its head. That's not to say that antidepressants are ineffective or shouldn't be taken, because for many people – myself included – antidepressant medication has been a pivotal part of finding ease and safety within. What it does do, however, is take so much weight from the shoulders of those who've been heavy with the label of 'chemically imbalanced' for part, or most, of their lives.

That being said, I don't disagree that there is some kind of imbalance when it comes to our experience of anxiety disorders. Just not the chemical sort. Rather, I think the imbalance lies in our aversion to discomfort, and our desire to make our moment-to-moment experience neat and tidy and free from tension or stress – even necessary tension or stress.

When I first learnt about the fight or flight response and the sympathetic nervous system, I remember feeling frustrated and disheartened by the existence of such a system. I read that, in days of the caveman, the fight or flight response was a fundamental and useful means of survival, whereas in the 21st century (when we no longer need to protect ourselves against man-eating predators) it's not nearly as vital. Since my fight or flight response seemed to trigger all of the time, I longed to have a way to turn it off permanently, so that it would stop disrupting my ability to function and live.

In reality, though, our need to feel aroused, alert and ready is just as important for our daily life as our need to feel calm and relaxed. You need your sympathetic nervous system for excitement, for sex, for energy, and to truly interact with the external environment. You need your parasympathetic nervous system for sex too, as well as for going inward, to disengage with the external environment, and to feel peaceful and relaxed enough to do basic things like urinating or defecating. It is when our systems are all working together that we are able to live and thrive; our entire life on this planet is a continuous, delicate balance – a relationship between opposing sides.

Our body is always seeking balance, and it will work with our mind in order to restore it, if we make that our goal. In the words of the 13th century poet and Sufi mystic, Rumi: *What you seek is seeking you.*

Despite anxiety disorders being the most common mental disorders in the developed world today (it is estimated that 1 in 13 people are suffering from some kind of an anxiety disorder), there is still much uncertainty surrounding what causes them in the first place. It appears that they develop over time, and there are a number of contributing factors. These include environmental factors (traumatic events, abuse, difficult family relationships, changes in work or school), underlying medical conditions (heart disease, thyroid problems, diabetes, etc.) and genetics.

However, it's important to note that anxiety disorders have a heritability of only 30 per cent. This means that just because someone in your family suffered from an anxiety disorder, it doesn't necessarily mean you are bound to that same genetic fate. The science of epigenetics is showing more and more that genes can be turned off or on, depending on a number of external factors. You may just as easily develop anxious behaviours that have been modelled to you by a caregiver, as you might because you share DNA with them. When it comes to the question of nature v nurture, the answer is 'a little of both'.

It's what you do now that has the power to change
where you're headed, not where you've been.

Personally speaking, I have no idea what caused me to start having panic attacks in the first place, and I'm genuinely at peace with the understanding that I may never know. Over the years, therapists have often asked me if there's anything that I think may have contributed to my anxiety disorder. This always feels like a trick question, because really, that's what I'm waiting for them to tell me! My answer is always the same: *Who knows?* There were big events that shook me, small events that prickled away at me, and there were the incremental moments in between where maybe I carried too much or thought too hard or smoked too often and slept too little.

Ultimately, regardless of the initial cause, if the behaviours that perpetuate the anxiety remain the same – such as resistance to fear and discomfort, patterns of unconscious behaviour, fighting or repressing – then the sense of disorder will also remain the same. The past has been and gone, for better or worse. We cannot time travel, or cherrypick events from our lives to remove from our memory. (And honestly, if we could time travel, the first thing I'd do would be go back to 2001 when I had my first date ever, and take back that accidental fart.)

That's not to say that the events which lead up to you being here now are unimportant or invaluable – not by any means. What I am saying is that spending all of your time and energy trying to pinpoint the beginning is energy more or less wasted on events that have already passed. It's what you do now that has the power to change where you are headed, not where you've been.

CHAPTER 4
THE IMPRINT OF PANIC

The sacred has a rough surface.

- Heather Mackay Young, Scottish poet and healer

– Although I find it helpful to understand anxiety from a biological perspective, it's still only half the picture. It's just as important to acknowledge and validate the emotional effect that panic and anxiety can imprint upon you.

I don't think it's a stretch to describe a panic attack as a type of trauma. Emotional trauma can be defined as 'an experience that leaves you feeling deeply unsafe or helpless', and a panic attack is certainly that. Experiencing a panic attack – whether for the first time or the fiftieth time – can cause you to feel like you don't know yourself, you can't trust yourself, and you very nearly died but have no idea why, or how to prevent it from happening again.

Before I'd experienced a panic attack for myself, I'm somewhat ashamed to say that I'd never really thought much about them. But to be fair, I hadn't really heard a lot about them. If someone had mentioned to me that they'd had a panic attack, I would've probably lumped it in the same category as a general feeling of anxiety, or perhaps some kind of emotional meltdown. If pressed, I'd probably have said that a panic attack was a moment of being very worried and maybe breathless and scared.

I mean … 'yes' and 'no'. It's almost comical how from the outside, it can appear that someone experiencing a panic attack is just having a moment where it's hard to catch their breath. These days, my panic attacks seem to pass by without being noticed by anyone outside of myself (although my eldest daughter always seems to know). But a panic attack feels like nothing you've experienced before – breathlessness is the least of your worries, when it feels like your entire body is shutting down, limb by limb, organ by organ.

⌖

The panic attack that preluded my anxiety diagnosis from the doctor was one that sent me to the emergency room in the middle of the night. Lying across my bed, scrolling mindlessly on my phone when I should have been asleep, I suddenly noticed that it was difficult to take a breath. As I became more aware (and more panicked) by my shallow breathing, I also noticed that I could no longer feel my feet. My legs were starting to tingle too, as if they were about to go completely numb. I couldn't breathe. All of a sudden, I was gasping for air.

Realising that something was very wrong, I yelled out to my dad. Within a matter of minutes, we were in the car and on our way to the nearest hospital. Dad rubbed my shoulders during the car ride, telling me it would be okay. But there was nothing about it that was okay. I remember thinking in that moment, 'Oh no, I've actually *shit myself*,' because if I couldn't feel the lower half of my body, how could I possibly hold on?

As we pulled into the emergency department carpark, I apologised profusely to the triage nurses who were helping me out of the car. I was certain that I was covered in my own faeces and everyone was going to see it. My skin burned with humiliation.

As it turned out, I hadn't shit myself, so I wasn't covered in my own faeces. But even if that had been the case, I don't think anyone would have batted an eyelid. After being bustled into the emergency ward, checked over and answered questions, the medical staff determined that I didn't require urgent attention (or really any attention at all) and I was left on a bed in a waiting bay, with dad checking in on me at intervals. Several long hours later, I was declared to be completely fine and promptly discharged. Apparently, there was nothing wrong with me.

This should have been a relief (and I'm sure for it was for Dad). But for me, it was the opposite. I felt more afraid than ever, because if what had just happened to me fell under the category of 'completely fine', then *what the hell was going on?*

When something happens to you that shakes you to your core – something you don't understand and can't explain, something that appears to be imaginary yet simultaneously is the most visceral experience you've ever had – of course, *of course*, it leaves a mark. When it happens repeatedly (as in the case of anxiety disorders), it worries away at you, impressing itself into the lines above your brow, drawing your chest in and raising your defences.

These episodes, when they remain an unknown but constant happening, create a dark space in your psyche that you become terrified of revisiting. This dark space is beyond lonely, because whenever you go there, not only are you are lost to everyone else, but you come back more and more lost to yourself.

Each panic attack I had, especially in those early days, felt like it was removing pieces of me. The despair I felt when trying unsuccessfully to communicate what I was going through – hearing myself describing my symptoms as if they were something I could accurately put into words. The exasperation of feeling like a burden on other people's time, energy and resources, of wishing my world would implode either a little bit quieter or loud enough to be heard by someone other than me. The fear. Oh my goodness – *the fear*. It never went away. All of this added together to subtract me from my own life, until I was nothing more than a dark place where a person used to be.

⚡

*Each panic attack I had, especially in those early days,
felt like it was removing pieces of me.*

⚡

But … there are some things that I've learned about the dark. I've learned that it's never as scary as it seems. When we shrink away from it, that's when it feels overwhelming. I've learned that darkness requires us to expand, in order to fully adjust. It requires us to breathe, to soften. If we allow our eyes the time to adapt, things become far clearer than we originally thought. Among the shadows and the shapes and the things we can't yet make out, there are tiny pockets of light.

So really, there are two aspects to the anxiety story. First, there is the fear response: chemicals and hormones, instincts and evolutionary design. And then there is the way we identify with and experience the fear response, which can result in trauma, emotional wounding and a pervasive sense of separation.

But … what about the multidimensional souls that these chemicals and hormones travel through? What about the human beings that have been the home for this trauma, those wounds? It's true that those imprints of panic shape us in an undeniable way, but it is in acknowledging this that we can explore ourselves more completely. Once we are willing to inspect these imprints, to trace a fingertip across their deep grooves and crevices, we are able to learn more about the journey that our hearts and souls have taken.

My panic attacks over the years have been grim, gut-clenching moments full of despair and shame and torment; yet they have also been tear-filled, heart-opening moments, moments that seemed to open me more fully to the world around me. Moments that acted as a catalyst for surrender – a call to stop clinging so tightly to control.

I used to worry that these imprints were imperfections. An accumulation of mental scars and wounds that rendered me disfigured, unworthy, undesirable. What I discovered though, is that these imprints were really pathways towards true vulnerability. Channels for the light to run through.

So I want you to know that I do understand wholeheartedly the impact that panic can have on your life. And because of this, I know just how much depth and beauty there is within you. It is because I understand the impact of panic that I also understand the impact of turning towards it, instead of continuously turning away.

It is because I've been to those dark places that I know just how much value there is to be found there … and how profoundly your life can (and will) change, if you decide to open yourself up to it.

CHAPTER 5
WHAT ARE YOU SO AFRAID OF?

I'm not afraid of death;
I just don't want to be there when it happens.
- Woody Allen, American filmmaker

- By the time I'd been housebound for the better part of a year, most of my friends were aware that I was suffering from an anxiety disorder. I'd been candid with my closest friends – often in the form of midnight text messages, bemoaning the situation I'd found myself in – but less forthcoming with co-workers and acquaintances. Even so, the conversations I had surrounding my inability to leave the house were few and far between. Except for my conversations with Jack.

Jack and I had known each other for years. A carpenter by trade and a perpetual optimist, Jack was quite possibly one of the most rational, logical people you could ever meet. Because of this, he was equal parts fascinated and frustrated by the imaginary force field that stopped me from walking out my front door.

One afternoon, we were having yet another brainstorming session in which he would present 'cures' for my disorder, and I'd shoot them down. (For example, Jack: *What if I just threw you in my car and drove you to the other side of Melbourne with no notice? Me: I would absolutely kill you!*) Then Jack asked me the one question that cut straight to the core of it all.

"I just don't get it," he sighed, referring to my refusal to go outside with him. "You know me. You know you're safe with me. *What is it that you're actually afraid of?*"

That was it. That was the million-dollar question.

What was I afraid of?

There were just so many things, I didn't know where to start. 'Having a panic attack' was the most obvious answer, because it was the one that most people seemed to understand, on some level or other.

Secretly though, and far more insidiously, the things I found myself most afraid of were the following: having a panic attack so vivid and distressing that I went insane, completely losing touch with reality. Humiliating myself. Doing something embarrassing. Yelling out without realising I was doing so. Being seen as disgusting or weird or strange. And, god ... that feeling of not being able to escape.

And yet, explaining that these were my fears didn't seem to adequately account for just how afraid I was. Because when I followed the thread of my fears, unravelled and disentangled them to pinpoint the one thing I was really, truly afraid of ... that one thing that seemed to eclipse all others was *fear itself.*

It wasn't always that way, fear and me. I can remember having a very healthy relationship with fear during the earlier years of my life. In fact, in a lot of ways, I used to enjoy feeling scared. My favourite movie as a kid was *Jaws*, because I loved the creepy music that played at the beginning, and the goosebumps that would prickle my skin when I heard the 'da dum'. While I was swimming around in our backyard pool, I would even pretend that I was being stalked by an enormous great white shark, and that any second I was going to be dragged under the water and eaten alive. (While typing this, I'm questioning whether this obsession was, in fact, 'healthy'.)

As a teenager I loved to do dangerous, fear-inducing things like going on midnight hikes with my mates in the dark forest of the state-park, or rollerblading down the tallest hill I could find, often setting up jumps and obstacles along the way, tempting fate to provide a broken leg or an impressive battle scar at the very least. My sister and I used to play a game with our next-door neighbours literally called *Scaredies*, which was more or less our take on the classic game *Murder in the Dark*, except that our version was less of a whodunnit, and more about just scaring each other stupid. The premise of the game was that two of us would try and hide together somewhere in the backyard at night, and the other two would have to find where we were hiding. They'd creep up silently, and then scream in our faces as loudly as possible. I loved that game.

You get the idea though. I wasn't scared of being scared – I relished it. The sensation of fear prickling up and down my spine was exhilarating. The adrenaline rush I got from being terrified was fun. And yet years later, the sensation of fear became one that would mentally and emotionally paralyse me.

The Emotion of Fear

For those of us with an anxiety disorder, fear is an emotion that seems to bookend our existence. We wake up covered in it, and we fall asleep drowning in it. I've often referred to the times I was housebound as the times I was 'fear-bound', because really, that's what it felt like. It was as if I were tied up in an invisible thread by everything I was afraid of. All I could think, see, hear and feel was fear.

Candace Pert, PhD and author of *Molecules of Emotion*[5], explained that what we feel as an emotion is actually the release of peptides travelling throughout the body, carrying with them an electrical charge. Emotions are then, quite literally, energy in motion. The root of the word 'emotion' is the Latin word *emovere*, meaning 'to move'. Each one of us has experienced an emotion moving through our body – from the way your heart swells when you look at someone you love, or the smile that breaks out across your face when you hear something really funny, or the sharp, short gasps and heaves that follow a fit of tears.

I can vividly remember being at my grandfather's funeral, walking away from his coffin completely unable to control the primal sobs and humiliating snorts erupting from some-where deep in my core – my whole rib cage was wracked with grief. I think of grief as the most exhausting of all emotions; it seems to take every ounce of your energy as it travels up and out.

Emotions are designed to initiate movement that will enable a return to equilibrium[6]. This means that it's in the feeling and expressing of emotions that we are able to return to a state of wholeness. When it comes to chronic fear, however, the emotion hasn't been allowed to move through us – we've felt the fear bubble up, but then we've held it there.

I think that part of the reason we do this is that, for many of us, the fear simply doesn't make sense. When we can't make sense of an emotion, how can we fully express it? And so the fear keeps popping back up – often at the most inopportune moments – just waiting to be released. And we keep trying to contain it, constricting ourselves tighter and tighter, trying to stop all that fear from exploding through our body. (It's here that the phrase 'pull yourself together' comes to mind.) Then, like a bottle of soda that has been shaken up repeatedly, we are so full to bursting with fear that we don't dare open the lid, even a little.

When we continually repress an emotion, it becomes locked in the body. Candace Pert explained it like this:

A feeling sparked in our mind or body will translate as a peptide being released somewhere. [Organs, tissues, skin, muscle and endocrine glands], they all have peptide receptors on them and can access and store emotional information. This means the emotional memory is stored in many places in the body, not just (or even primarily) in the brain ... I think unexpressed emotions are literally lodged in the body. The real true emotions that need to be expressed are in the body, trying to move up and be expressed and thereby integrated, made whole, and healed.[7]

When we can't make sense of an emotion, how can we fully express it?

If you've ever woken up in the morning and felt your skin prickle with that familiar cold sweat – a deep sense of trepidation, before you've even really opened your eyes – you'll know what it feels like to have fear trapped in the body. If you've ever stood in the shower and sobbed because stepping out and getting dressed seemed utterly pointless, you'll know what it feels like to have fear trapped in the body. If you've sat in your car ready to turn on the ignition – a simple act that so many do without thinking – while your entire body screams at you to give up, to go back inside – you know what it's like to have fear trapped in the body.

The human body is not designed to live in a chronic state of fear. Again, fear is an emotion that is supposed to be released – not unconsciously held on to and stoked like a fire. It takes a lot of energy to live in constant fear, and the effects on the body can be toxic. At the 2017 Neuroscience Education Institute (NEI) Congress, chronic fear was linked to multiple mental and physical health conditions, including chronic fatigue, metabolic disorders (e.g., diabetes, obesity), depression, compromised immune function, migraines, fibromyalgia, chronic pain, asthma and eating disorders.[8]

For me, living in chronic fear meant that I would wake up in the morning with an aching jaw from grinding my teeth all night. My irritable bowel syndrome (IBS) flared constantly (which would increase my anxiety, further aggravating my IBS in a vicious, bloated cycle), my weight went up and down like a yoyo, and I was never in the mood for sex. Who wants to have sex when they always feel like they're dying? Not me.

And it was always there – that feeling. Both a sense of inescapable fear, and a constant searching for it. A need to find it, and an even more desperate need to get rid of it. It didn't matter what I was doing, or where I was, or who I was with ... it always felt like the world was ending.

There is a misconception that agoraphobics stay at home because it's the only place we feel safe, but truthfully, I didn't feel safe anywhere at all. I stayed home because home was where I could best control my unease. There was less risk of judgement when I was at home, because I was home alone the majority of the time. But even at home, in the place that was most familiar to me, I still felt terrified, I still felt unsafe, I still felt acutely uneasy in my own body. This was what made me feel so abnormal and left me convinced that I was never going to get better. I felt the fear everywhere. It was an ongoing tension, a clutching around my chest, a sinking in the pit of my stomach.

Candace Pert likened our emotions to music, stating that we are "like a tuning fork" – constantly vibrating, cells rhythmically communicating with one another. My body had become a complete symphony of fear – a cacophony of deafening noises and sensations that set my teeth on edge. I would wonder if everyone felt this way, and if they did, how on earth did they manage to get on with life? I remember trying to explain it to my family, telling them how hard everything had become. I was putting so much energy into just trying to get through the day, my body physically ached from exertion, even when I was sitting around doing nothing.

Eventually, I stopped attempting to explain how I felt, because it didn't change anything. None of the advice given to me seemed to work, and I felt as if I were constantly complaining; even I was tired of hearing myself. And so I screwed the lid on tighter. Held it in.

It was this 'holding it in' that changed me the most. I went from being open to life to being completely closed off. When all of your strength is going towards keeping yourself together, you forget how to let go, and you become rigid. Clinical psychologist, meditation teacher and author Tara Brach put it beautifully when she said: "As we tense in anticipation of what may go wrong, our heart and mind contract. We forget that there are people who care about us, and about our own ability to feel spacious and openhearted."[9]

My ex-boyfriend put it somewhat less beautifully when he told me wearily, "You used to be fun. You used to say 'yes' to things. Now you say 'no' before I've even finished asking the question."

He was right, and I hated him for it. Before agoraphobia and panic, I was fun. I was always keen for an adventure. But now, I had changed so much I could barely stand it. I was exhausted by my own bullshit. I didn't recognise the girl looking back at me in the mirror. I resented myself for not being 'strong'. For letting those fears take over my life. I'd spit at myself: *Why can't you just be normal? What is wrong with you?*

Chronic fear also changes how you relate to yourself. You become distrustful of your body, of its signals and sensations (more on this in Chapter 17). You become terrified of your thoughts and your own mind. You lose yourself among the chatter, among the what-ifs. Where there was once an eagerness and a willingness to experience life, now exists an abandonment of possibility.

The most unfortunate part, of course, is that when this chronic undercurrent of fear goes on unchecked for long enough, you start to believe that this is just the way you are. This is your life now – you'll always have this feeling inside you, gurgling away in your stomach, burning at the back of your neck. Fear no longer becomes an emotion but a behaviour, a personality trait. You are always terrified, and you are terrified of just how terrified you are. It's the perfect storm, and to live there is to be perpetually cold and wet, drowning in the dark.

Here's the good news though: *This is **not** the way you are.*

CHAPTER 6
THE WEIGHT OF FEAR

– There is a story of a teacher who holds up a glass of water in front of her class, and asks them, "How heavy do you think this glass of water is?"

The answers vary; some students believe the glass of water weighs a few hundred grams or so, others think it must be closer to a kilogram. They are quiet for a few moments, each of them trying to figure out the maths – how heavy is the glass itself, minus the liquid? How much does a few hundred millilitres of water weigh?

The teacher finally tells the class, "From my perspective, the absolute weight of this glass doesn't matter. It all depends on how long I hold it. If I hold it for a minute or two, it's fairly light. If I hold it for an hour straight, its weight might make my arm ache a little. If I hold it for a day, my arm will likely cramp up and feel completely numb and paralysed, forcing me to drop the glass to the floor. In each case, the weight of the glass doesn't change, but the longer I hold it, the heavier it feels to me."

She continued, "Your stresses and worries in life are very much like this glass of water. Think about them for a while and nothing happens. Think about them a bit longer and you begin to ache a little. Think about them all day long, and you will feel completely numb and paralysed – incapable of doing anything else until you drop them."

I love this story; it illustrates so well how the emotions we repress can take over our lives. The longer you have repressed and held on to your fears, the heavier and more paralysing those fears have become. You may have held those fears for months, years. Decades even. You may have been holding onto those fears as tightly as possible, every single second of the day. Maybe even in your sleep.

Think now, of one of your strongest fears. Maybe you fear going crazy or losing control of your body, like I did. Maybe you fear becoming sick, always watching for a drop in your blood sugar or a change in your heart rate. Maybe you're terrified that you'll pass out or need to go to hospital, leaving your loved ones to fend for themselves.

Whatever that fear is for you, bring it to the forefront of your consciousness for a moment. Was there a time when this fear wasn't as prevalent? When it didn't consume your thoughts from morning till night? Perhaps your fear started out as a fleeting thought – a jarring possibility that came up during a moment of distress and, because it was so startling, you held it there. Worrying at it. Inspecting it from every angle; trying your hardest not to think about it by thinking about it constantly. Perhaps your fear has even come to life at one point or another, and that's why you can feel it so vividly. The body remembers fear viscerally, unlike the mind.

The interesting thing about the fears we hold onto is that, although consciously we wish we could stop carrying the fear, stop letting it roll around in our bones and our blood … unconsciously, we still want to keep it very much at the heart of everything we do. Because if we don't, how are we protecting ourselves against it? How are we stopping it from happening? This continuous push and pull, this need to prevent an occurrence by worrying about it, visualising it, imagining it, living it on the inside to avoid it on the outside … this is what exhausts us.

It's not the content of our fear that is the scariest thing, as much as we'd like to believe otherwise. It's the weight, the burden of carrying something inside for so damn long, when all we ever needed to do was just let it go.

So, let me ask you this. If you could let go of this fear, and I mean really let it go … would you? And if by letting it go, that meant you weren't actively trying to prevent it, would you still do it? Would you put it down, release it into the ether, allow it to be a possibility completely out of your control?

It's okay if your answer isn't 'yes', by the way. The value lies more in the question than the answer, in the willingness to explore the idea that the thing you've been so afraid of might not be worth the space you've given it in your body and mind. The more willing you are to walk in that direction, the closer you will be to learning how to let that fear go.

⇌

It's important to remember that, by its very nature, fear is designed to cause a reaction within us. It is supposed to energise us, to invigorate, to awaken. It's supposed to make us feel breathless, alive and intense. Of course, for those of us with an anxiety disorder, those are feelings that we tend to run away from. This means that allowing yourself to feel fear, in order to release it, is going to feel uncomfortable. There is no denying that. When we turn away from that truth, when we resist it and avoid it and refuse it, this is when fear stagnates and becomes like the glass of water that we've been holding up for days, weeks and years on end.

Conversely, when we turn towards that truth, when we step forward with knocking knees, we enable fear to travel out of our mind and physical body. I am sure you can think of a time when you were terrified of doing something that you really wanted to do, and when you did it, even though you were scared, you felt a weight lifted from within. It is a very physical release; it tingles and shakes through us, bringing blood to our cheeks. This is the true sensation of fear. Not the burden. Not the heaviness.

For the first time in a long time, I was relating differently to my fear, and it felt uncomfortable and unfamiliar ... but it also felt alive.

When I first started doing exposure therapy (and I use the term 'exposure therapy' loosely, as what I was doing was going outside for as long as I could stand, and then going back and doing it again the next day), I remember feeling so scared, so anxious, so petrified of what might happen. I remember asking myself: *When will this get easier? When will it feel different? When will I finally stop being afraid?*

What I didn't realise at the time was that this was my body learning how to outwardly process fear, and I wasn't used to that. I was used to internalising the fear, storing it in my body for safekeeping (or rather, for keeping myself safe). Now I was using it, feeling it, releasing it. I was letting it bubble out through my skin, instead of trying to swallow it down. For the first time in a long time, I was relating differently to my fear, and it felt uncomfortable and unfamiliar. But it also felt alive. I finally felt alive.

I know that you have spent so much time worrying about your fears, thinking of all the things that you wish you could do, but cannot do because you are afraid, and I know you are desperate to be able to do them. It is not for lack of wanting that you are here, now. But what I can tell you for certain is this: waiting for your fears to subside so that you can get out there is not the way it works. Your fears will subside along with the movement. The only way you disentangle yourself from the fear of losing control, passing out, going to hospital or whatever it is that you have been so terrified of – is to consciously move towards that possibility. And what you'll discover along the way is that those fears were never yours to hold.

CHAPTER 7

THE PATH OF MOST RESISTANCE

– For many of us, our young adult years are spent in an experimental phase. We explore different styles, different partners, different career choices. It's a time of constant redirection, as we navigate our way forwards on our chosen path.

For me, my experimental phase was made up of one experiment only: how long could I go on pretending to move forwards while staying perfectly still. I thought I was doing a pretty good job of it too. Although I was still confined to my house, my boyfriend and I were expecting our first baby – a little girl. I was undertaking a bachelor's degree via an online university, making my way through meaty assignments and lengthy essays in my 'spare time', which I had in abundance. I regularly discussed things like renovating the kitchen or laundry, or moving house altogether, as if these were possibilities in my immediate future that required my thoughtful attention.

In reality though, I was the opposite of a duck in water. Looking extremely busy on the surface but doing absolutely nothing underneath. My relationship was falling apart at the seams. I was doing a degree simply to buy myself time – trying to fill the endless hours with something of substance, acting like I had a career path in mind, when I really didn't have a clue. And as for moving house or renovating? Given that I was living in my parents' house, which they had very kindly moved out of when it became clear to everyone that I wasn't going anywhere, I wasn't any more likely to renovate than I was to take a trip to the moon.

I was living in the most glaring state of arrested development but doing my darnedest to ignore the signs. It was like when kids play 'house', except I wasn't a kid. Instead of playing house, I was playing at having a life.

Part of me knew that I couldn't keep it up forever. There was, of course, the very time-sensitive issue of the baby I was soon to birth, and for that I'd have to at least leave the house in order to get to a hospital. I also knew that it was unlikely my relationship would survive much longer, if the only place we were 'in a relationship' was at home. By that stage, my boyfriend had become used to attending everything on his own and offering vague apologies as to why I wasn't there. (Truthfully, I don't even know if he did offer apologies; I'm sure there was a point when people stopped expecting me to show up.)

Up until falling pregnant, I had uncomfortably existed in a space of being so dysfunctional that I couldn't work or socialise or do anything 'normal', but not so dysfunctional that I couldn't go through the motions of waking up and passing the hours until bedtime. But then, with the impending arrival of my daughter and the pressure mounting to finally 'overcome' agoraphobia – as opposed to just talking about it – I started to tip further into the realm of non-functional, edging closer and closer to losing it completely.

━

I remember one day in particular, when I woke up not knowing if I was real anymore. Was I awake? Was I really here? If I screamed out right now, would it make a sound? I kept scrunching my fingers into my palms, digging my nails into my flesh, trying to somehow create enough physical pain to expel the distress from inside my body. I spent the day curled up in a ball in my ensuite bathroom, sitting on the closed toilet lid in despair, not knowing what to do with myself.

I rang my doctor and tried to explain how terrified I was – that my anxiety had become so unbearable and intense that I could feel it in my *teeth* – but his words of encouragement barely made a dent in the static of my mind. Everything he said seemed like it was coming from a different world, meant for a different version of me. Why could no one reach me here? Why couldn't I get anyone to understand what I was going through, without sounding overly dramatic or insane?

Didn't these people understand that I was completely falling apart? I didn't want to have to keep explaining myself. I didn't want to be alone. I didn't want to keep complaining about how hard it all was, but I also didn't want it to be so f**king hard.

I didn't want to be housebound, agoraphobic, anxious or depressed anymore. But … I didn't want to do the things that scared me, in order to overcome all of that.

I was wedged beneath so much of what I didn't want that I felt flattened by my own demands. It became clear to me that I had successfully made my world so tiny, so controlled and so uninhabitable, that there was nowhere left to go. That corner of the ensuite was all I had left, and even there, I still didn't feel safe.

I think that there comes a breaking point – especially with agoraphobia – where you realise that although you've avoided and resisted and done everything possible to stay firmly within your comfort zone, you are still completely terrified. You become aware that every strategy you've employed until that point to keep yourself safe has only resulted in you feeling the most unsafe you've ever felt. And now, resisting and avoiding your fears is not so much a choice or a preference, but a jail in which you are locked.

It's a startling realisation when you finally acknowledge that you are more resistance than person. More 'no' than 'yes'. When you acknowledge that you have exhausted all your energy trying to avoid the things you don't want, only to find that as a result *you are what you don't want*.

The most common response to anxiety – and indeed, to any unpleasant feelings or emotions – is resistance. We resist feeling bad on all levels. Collectively, we are programmed to do this, both through our need to avoid discomfort, and through the messages we receive from well-meaning caregivers and society in general about what is acceptable and what isn't. We've all seen a child take a tumble and, before they can even begin to cry, their parent immediately brushes it off and says (in that singsong voice), 'You're okay!'

I do this all the time with my kids, without intending to. It's almost a reflex. Minimise the pain. Avoid the tears. It's natural for a parent to want to do this, as much as for anyone; we don't want the people we love to be in pain, nor do we want that pain for ourselves. And so we try to turn the other way. Move away from hurt and move towards happiness, pleasure, comfort, okayness.

The problem with resisting anxiety is that it's the resistance that increases the anxiety; it makes it more prevalent, more all-encompassing, more deeply entrenched in our bones. When we are trying to avoid something, we train ourselves to be on the lookout for it. We then become so obsessed with trying to find and avoid the uncomfortable feelings that we become completely stuck in them. Much like the weight of repressed fear, if we aren't willing to face and feel our unpleasant emotions then, sooner or later, we end up drowning in them.

We used to play this game at the arcade when we were kids, where you had to whack plastic crocodiles on the snout with a foam mallet. The crocodiles would pop out slowly, one at a time, and you'd settle into a smug kind of confidence as you managed, quite easily, to whack each one before it went back into its hole. But when level two kicked in and a mechanical croc voice declared, "Now I'm *really* angry!", you'd suddenly have crocodiles popping up all over the place. Unless you had a second player on standby to assist in croc-whacking, you'd be done for. Game over.

I'd somehow found myself living out my own strange version of that croc-whacking game: trying desperately to hold everything I ever wanted in my hands – a healthy, happy pregnancy, a good relationship, a social life, a house with a white picket fence – while also trying to whack every occurrence of panic and fear square on the head, all popping up faster and faster, again and again and again, until I just couldn't do it anymore. It was game over; I had no lives left.

You see, that's the irony in resistance: when you are so hell-bent on trying to remove the things that scare you, you don't have the resources to hold onto the things that are genuinely important to you at the same time. You simply can't do both. And so you begin to lose, one by one, each and everything that is important and valuable to you, because you are so deeply focused on trying to avoid and resist the things that make you anxious.

After my daughter was born, my need to keep resisting discomfort and fear collided heavily with my need to love and care for my baby to the best of my ability. Among the fog of new motherhood, trying to steer myself through sleepless nights, endlessly fluctuating hormones and the jarring shock of being totally responsible for a human being other than myself, it quickly became apparent that I wasn't going to be able to keep turning myself away from anxiety. Nor was I going to be able to skip ahead to the part where I was 'recovered', avoiding the unwanted and charging straight towards all the good.

Motherhood is one of those strange, wonderful experiences that strips you down to your core. It's messy. It's raw. It's the lowest of lows and the highest of highs, all clashing together in the exact same moments.

Maybe that was just what I needed: to see how something can be the hardest thing you've ever done but also the most beautiful, the most rewarding and the most transformative all at once. I needed to know that those states could coexist – that fear and love, joy and pain, hope and despair were all relevant, necessary and equal aspects of my experience.

Don't get me wrong – I still tried hard to hold on to the shreds of resistance that I had left. By that stage, pulling away was so ingrained in me that it was an automatic reflex. For example, when it came time to leave the hospital with my newborn baby, I asked Mum to drive me home in another car, while my boyfriend came home with our daughter. I sat in the back seat, headphones firmly stuck in my ears, with a blanket over my head. I was so frightened of being in the car with someone else that I quite literally *couldn't bear to look.*

When I received an invitation to a community mothers' group to meet other mums in my suburb, I initially refused to go. The meeting spot was a seven-minute walk from home – less than a two-minute drive – but I maintained that I was too anxious for something like that. Who needed mothers' groups, anyway?

I sent my baby off for her first immunisations with her dad, again assuming that it would be something too anxiety-provoking for me, not wanting to bring my own 'drama' into the room, when the important thing was getting her vaccinated. At least, that's what I told my boyfriend as I buttoned up our daughter's tiny jacket, buckled her into the car seat and waved her goodbye.

But as I watched them pull out of the driveway, it all started to crumble. These little acts of pulling away from the world started to pull away at me. I wasn't just failing myself anymore. I was failing my baby too. How could I send her off to get a needle jabbed into her thigh, without me being there to comfort her when she cried? How could I deprive her of social interaction with other babies, just because I was afraid of meeting other mums? How could I keep on refusing to be present in my life, when my life now had her in it?

It's weird and disconcerting that we can spend so long complaining about how difficult and painful something is, without realising that the real difficulty lies in how unwilling we are to break away from it. The pain gets dragged out because we are wrapping ourselves in it; we are reliving it endlessly, as if there is no other choice. This reminds me of the sheep that we had on our property growing up; they would occasionally get stuck in the muddy bog if there had been a lot of rain. Even when my dad tried to drag them out of the bog, they'd just stand there. Stuck. Refusing to move. Refusing to be helped.

My friend Rachel[10], who navigated five years of being housebound due to severe panic attacks and overwhelming anxiety, put it like this: *I was miserable but I was comfortable, because I was certain of what each day would bring.*

We convince ourselves – to our detriment – that we are bound by anxiety. That we have no option but to avoid and control, because what's waiting for us on the other side is going hurt more than we can bear. We whisper this reasoning to ourselves, over and over and over again, until we are breathless and blue, not understanding that if we stopped repeating our limitations for just one moment we'd finally have time to breathe.

CHAPTER 8

THE WAYS WE RESIST

– I learnt very quickly that there are all sorts of ways that we resist feeling anxious. These range from the more active, obvious forms of resistance such as complete avoidance, to the more subtle, passive forms of resistance such as safety behaviours, defending our position (also known as 'victim mentality') and procrastination.

The common theme with all forms of resistance is that they come at a huge cost to our mental, physical and spiritual wellbeing, both in the short term and more severely in the long term. I'm going to break down each form of resistance in this chapter. Whether you see yourself in one or more of them, please know that it doesn't matter how long you have spent in resistance, you can always choose a different path.

Avoidance

Avoidance is the favourite flavour of the agoraphobe. When you're so terrified of leaving your house for fear of what happens to your body and brain when you do so, it makes sense to avoid leaving your house altogether. The interesting thing about avoidance on this level is that it's not so much a conscious decision as a deeply ingrained safety mechanism.

Perhaps the most obvious cost of avoidance is missing out (on everything!) and life becoming extremely difficult. Even though we are well-equipped in this day and age to have everything delivered to us at home, there comes a time when you need to leave, and if you can't leave, then what do you do?

What often happens when it comes to avoidance is that what starts out as avoidance of a particular place, situation or person/people, quickly becomes an avoidance of everywhere, everyone and everything. From there, it's only a short matter of time before it's not just the act of going out that causes discomfort, but simply thinking about going out.

The cost of avoidance is that our discomfort grows in direct proportion to the shrinking of our comfort zone.

Engaging in Safety Behaviours

A safety behaviour/strategy is essentially avoidance with conditions attached: I will do X, but only if Y or Z happen. For example, going out only when you are with your 'safe person', or driving on local roads but avoiding freeways or high-traffic areas.

Some of my safety behaviours were only going out mid-afternoon – never in the morning – and making sure I always had a sweater tied around my waist, ensuring that if I did finally have that panic-induced diarrhoea attack I was so deeply afraid of, I could at least try to hide it.

The cost of this form of resistance is that not only do your safety behaviours tend to get more intense and quite bizarre over time (do you really need ten bottles of pills rattling around in your handbag, just to go down the street to the corner shop?), but this rigidity also prevents you from realising that you can indeed do the things you think you cannot do. You start to believe that the only reason you are able to do X was because of Y or Z. Putting such weight on items or other people to enable you to cope takes away from your own strength and resilience. The thing is, when it really comes down to it, we are far more capable than we give ourselves credit for.

Attempting to Control Everything

When our survival instinct is threatened, we feel safer if we can exert control over something. My dad displayed this often when my sister and I were teenagers. If there was some kind of fight or emotional meltdown happening between us, you would find him in the kitchen, doing the dishes – regardless of whether there were dishes to be done. It was almost as if he was saying, "I can't control or clean up your feelings, so I'll clean up the kitchen instead."

For those of us with heightened anxiety, the sense of feeling out of control in our internal world becomes so overwhelming that we try to exert as much control as possible over our external world. A big control issue for me was being a passenger in the car. I refused to be driven by anyone other than myself, because it meant that I wouldn't be in control of when we stopped or turned around. Even when I started to get more practised at sitting in the passenger seat, I would feel trapped and furious if the driver took a detour I wasn't prepared for, or asked if we could "just pop into the shops for a minute?" If I hadn't expected or planned for it, it wasn't happening.

This incessant need to control every facet of my life came at an enormous cost to both me and my relationships. I became a real pain in the ass to be around, because of how unwilling and inflexible I was. I also felt utterly depleted, every minute of the day. The reality of life is that it demands a level of fluidity from all of us, and I felt those demands pulling on me like a fast-moving river, dragging me under. Attempting to keep a tight hold on every single outcome was truly exhausting; it caused the greatest sense of suffering, because it ended up making it impossible for me to get anywhere at all.

The funny thing about control is that it really is an illusion. None of us have control – we never did. There are just so many variables, so many things changing all the time. The only permanent thing we have is the knowledge that everything is impermanent. The cost of always trying to exert control is that you will genuinely drive yourself crazy trying to do something that isn't possible in the first place. And the more you try to control, the more out of control you will feel. How does the saying go? Try to manage everything, and you end up managing nothing.

Self-Medication and Substance Abuse

This form of resistance is the most damaging. Drug, alcohol and food addiction/dependency are all very real, extremely insidious problems in and of themselves. When it comes to self-medicating or abusing substances in order to cope with anxiety, the biggest difficulty is that it becomes a cycle that feeds into itself. What starts out as a way to make you feel better ultimately ends up making you feel worse.

That glass of 'liquid courage' before an event might feel like it loosens your tongue enough to talk to strangers, but it also feels like cement in your veins the next day. That half of a sedative pill you take to deal with crippling panic somehow stops taking the edge off after a couple of months. Before long you're taking three at a time, just to feel capable of getting through the day.

The cost of self-medication and substance abuse is obvious: you are risking your health and your life every time you engage in this form of resistance. If this something that you struggle with, please know there is help available. Flip to the back of this book to find resources to help.

Procrastination

This is probably one of the more 'socially acceptable' forms of resistance, in that we pretty much all do it at some point or another. (I am a chronic procrastinator; take the *decade* I spent writing this book as proof!) What's most interesting about procrastination as a form of resistance is how it creates a soothing, false sense of security. But behind the curtain, it's making our worries and fears larger and seemingly more terrifying with every passing minute. Similar to control, it's illusory but feels much nicer.

I'll get to it eventually, just not right now.

I will do it, but I'm just not ready.

I still need to learn more, or read more, or practise more (insert totally valid excuse here) and then I'll do it.

And amazingly, we feel okay here in the 'one day'. The sense that we are going to do it eventually gets us through the reality that we are not doing it right now.

The way procrastination manifested for me, in terms of my anxiety, was that I knew that, at some point or other, I was going to have to do the things that frightened me. Of course I would. Eventually. Just not today, because today was a bad day for various reasons and I'd get to it tomorrow, okay?

I mistakenly assumed that there were more lessons I needed to learn, perhaps a level of 'stability' that I needed to reach with my medication, or just something that I didn't yet possess. But when I did, then I would get out there and do the scary things. And even when I did finally start leaving the house and engaging in my own forms of exposure therapy, I would procrastinate before heading out the door. Doing incredibly useless things like curling my hair, changing my outfit, taking photos to put on Instagram, anything that would prolong my safely staying ensconced within my comfort zone.

The glaring cost of procrastination as a form of resistance is that we never get where we want to be, because we're too busy saying that we'll do it tomorrow. But, as I've found time and time again, the most devastating result of chronic procrastination is a total loss of trust in yourself. When you consistently fail to keep your word to yourself, it feels like there is nobody in your corner. It doesn't necessarily mean you don't show up for others or that you are lazy. Many people who put themselves last do so because they put everyone else first. When I'm asked to do something for somebody else, I tend to get it done as soon as humanely possible (mostly because I'm terrified of disappointing others, but that's a whole other thing in itself).

When it comes to doing things for me, however, it's like I end up taking a permanent commercial break and then I feel hopeless, defeated and uncertain of my capabilities in any area of my life – whether relationships, work, health, finances and on it goes. I see other people creating goals and working away at them and I think to myself: *What's wrong with me? Why can't I break out of this rut? Why do I never work hard at what I need?* Nothing feels quite as empty as knowing that you have, on all levels, refused to show up for yourself.

We've all heard the phrase 'listen to your heart'. I truly believe that our hearts listen to us too. If there is something important that you really, truly want, but you continue to procrastinate before going after it, your heart will take note. It remembers being disregarded, it remembers your refusal to take seriously whatever you desire. Your relationship with yourself is the most important relationship you will ever have, and doing what you say you will do for yourself is an integral part of maintaining that relationship.

Defending Our Position

This form of resistance is the sneakiest one of all, and probably the hardest to take ownership of. Defending our position, also known as victim mentality, is when we constantly try to justify why things are as hard as they are. Some might call this 'making excuses', although I don't believe this to be the case. An excuse is usually something we know to be bullshit, and it's often how we try to cover ourselves when we know we're in the wrong. Defending our position is more nuanced, because the reasons we don't face our fears are not bullshit – they are valid, they are understandable, and they are often completely legitimate reasons (even if not completely rational).

The reasoning behind your perceived limitations may be entirely true. For example, you may truly have a fear of heights, or a fear of vomiting, or a fear of flying. I've witnessed my partner turn as white as a sheet during a flight on a very small plane, because he is genuinely terrified of enclosed spaces. That's not an excuse, that's a legitimate fear. But regardless of whether we have a legitimate reason for our limits, if we continually live in those truths as justification for why we cannot do something, that's when we are crossing the line from acceptance to resistance. That's when we are taking the path that leads nowhere fast.

There is a quote by Richard Bach which goes: "Argue for your limitations, and sure enough, they're yours."[11] This means, if you want to hold onto your ability to stay terrified, then by all means keep listing the reasons why you need to remain terrified. Even if they are completely valid reasons. Even if it makes sense. Even if it's completely understandable and no one would blame you for being terrified. Because the only person who benefits from your justifications is you – just not in any helpful, progressive way.

I have played the victim on countless occasions. It would start with something as simple as receiving an invitation for a birthday party. My brain would immediately start ticking over with all the reasons why I couldn't attend. I'd even be annoyed at whoever organised the party for actually inviting me – *don't they know how hard it is for me?* Even though there would be a little voice deep inside saying, *but ... maybe you could try?* it would be quickly drowned out by all the parts of me that needed to defend my desire to stay safe. And I'd overexplain it to family: "It's just going to be too hard, you know? I can't get there. I'd have to wake up too early and my IBS is never good in the mornings and it'll be too hot or too cold and Mercury is in retrograde and I haven't been out in years and it just won't work …" All the while not realising that it wasn't my family I was trying to convince, but me. It was me that I was trying to ease.

The cost of defending your position is that these entirely valid, entirely useless justifications end up like cement wrapped around your ankles. You become resentful of the world for asking so much of you, while keeping you pinned to the ground. How dare the universe require you to work through hardship? It's so unfair. So unjust. So *common*.

Because that's the truth, right there. Every single one of us walking this planet has a million reasons why it's hard to get out of bed in the morning. We forget about the beauty of the fact that we get to wake up at all. There will always be any number of truthful reasons why our fears are our fears and why facing them is hard. That won't ever change. What will change is the minutes we have left on this planet, and I don't know about you, but I don't want to spend them listing all the reasons why living is hard. I just want to spend them living.

※

We employ the above tactics of resistance in an attempt to find ourselves, to keep ourselves safe and calm, and to separate ourselves from the constant buzz of panic and pain. We do this, not realising that it's within these acts of resistance that we feel more panic and more pain. The more we resist, the more anxious we ultimately feel.

Resisting discomfort and fear also has a snowball effect. What starts out as a small strategy of avoidance becomes a tangled web of rules, coping behaviours and conditions that eventually consume you completely. It's exhausting and nearly impossible to have a life within the tiny cracks in which you allow yourself to exist.

The ultimate cost of resistance, in whatever shape or form, is that eventually you become fully disconnected from both yourself and the world around you. You detach from your soul, from your future, and from everything that is good in this life. For you cannot avoid the uncomfortable without also sacrificing the comfortable. You cannot avoid the bad without also sacrificing the good.

When I think of all the beautiful things I missed because I was too busy trying to dodge discomfort, my heart breaks. I found out the hard way that it doesn't take much for resistance towards anxiety to become a complete rejection of life.

*The more ways that we resist, the more
anxious we ultimately feel.*

I know how painful and gut-wrenching it is when you desperately want to live but are terrified of doing so. I know how upsetting it can be when it seems like everything you do (or cannot stop doing) is preventing you from being the person you want to be. But hear me when I tell you that it doesn't have to be this way; you are not as trapped as you may believe. In fact, the behaviours that seem to hold us back the most are entirely malleable, if only we are willing to try something new.

CHAPTER 9

THE HABIT OF BEING ANXIOUS

– *In the editorial feedback for* the first draft of this book, it was gently noted that there was a lot of repetition in my stories. Lots of talk about 'fear of shitting' and frustration with not being able to make it to the end of my street, at best. The notes weren't wrong; these were themes that came up again and again in my writing. Although some of that could be blamed on inexperience – this being my first ever book – I wanted to argue that the reason these themes came up again and again in my writing was because they came up again and again (and again!) in my real life.

I can't tell you how many mornings I've spent sitting in a bathroom, waiting for the nausea in my belly to abate. I can't tell you how many times I've rehearsed potential outcomes in my head, catastrophising to the nth degree in order to be absolutely certain that I can cope (always resulting in me being convinced that I cannot cope, and I should probably cancel). I can't tell you how many conversations I've checked out of, too distracted by the sweat pooling at the base of my spine to have any awareness of what words were being said. And the number of times I've stood up after peeing, only to sit back down on the toilet again to try and pee just that little bit more, because what if there is more in there? What if I need to wee again? Sit down, stand up, sit down, stand up.

I've disassociated, I've ruminated, I've turned the car around at the halfway point. I've postponed, I've avoided, I've left early or not shown up at all. I've spent hours upon hours scanning my body for discomfort – assessing my heartbeat, my breath, my tummy, my throat – hunting for something to freak out about and freaking out whether I found something or not.

I've done these things repeatedly, because this is the hallmark of a life with anxiety. These were my anxious behaviours, and these were the ways in which I was unwillingly tied to my disorder, and my disorder tied to me.

At least, so I thought.

One reason anxiety disorders feel so insurmountable – and why they seem to take over our lives – is the repetitive nature of the way we experience them. There's the mental and emotional obsessing, the recurrent intrusive thoughts, the overthinking, the overexplaining, the overpreparing. Everything is done to excess, and it is done again and again without our conscious prompting. Trapped on a merry-go-round of things we wish we didn't do, think or say, we can see a way of living that doesn't involve this cyclical dread, but we can't seem to get ourselves there. And by the time we become aware of our patterns of behaviour, we are already firmly cemented within them.

But this concept of repetition isn't just limited to anxiety disorders. Unconscious behaviour repetition is something we all do, for the very reason that human beings are wired for efficiency, and being able to repeat a behaviour with little conscious thought is the most efficient way of going about it. When we learn a behaviour or process and we repeat it a number of times, we encode it into the memory of our body. This means that the next time we need to act out the behaviour or process, we can do so unconsciously.

This is why your finger can punch in a sequence of numbers on a keypad, without you being able to consciously recall that sequence. This is why you can travel along a familiar route and realise afterwards that you don't remember most of the drive. This is why you can draw a blank when asked what you had for breakfast yesterday, whether you brushed your teeth this morning or took your pills last night. You're 90% sure you did – because you always do – but you can't consciously remember doing so. These are more obvious examples of our ability to perform an action without thinking about it, but the fact is that a scarily significant portion of our lives is not dictated by conscious thought in the moment but instead by our subconscious.

It's as if our body is dancing to a beat that only our subconscious mind can hear. We nearly always move through our day in much the same way we did the day before, doing things in the pattern to which we have become most familiar.

These familiar patterns then tend to take shape in the form of our identity. For example, we say "I'm a night owl", because we always stay up late. We say, "She's a fitness nut" about someone who works out every day. Or we say, "I'm an anxious person" because our waking moments are awash with angst and nerves and fear and worry, as well as behaviours that perpetuate much of the same.

We believe that this is who we are, because we are habitually acting in a way that reaffirms our anxiety.

The more we act out these habits, the more ingrained they are in the rhythm of our subconscious mind. We continue to dance to the same beat. And while we may desperately want to turn off the music, our body is going to keep going through the motions of what we know, even against our better judgement. To further exacerbate things, it is in those times when we are operating from survival mode that our body is likely to rely on what is familiar, as opposed to what is rational or most consciously desired. Studies have shown that when we are under chronic or acute stress, we default to our habitual patterning[12], perhaps as sort of a panacea, a way of soothing the fires within.

The Wanted vs The Known

Just as we can reinforce a behaviour or process into our subconscious, we can also encode the chemical signature of a thought, attitude or feeling. Whenever you think a particular thought, your brain releases chemical signals which cause the body to feel the same way as you are thinking. Dr Joe Dispenza, author of *Becoming Supernatural*, calls this the 'thinking and feeling loop', because what happens is that your body feels equal to the way you are thinking, and then you think equal to the way you are feeling. On and on it goes … thought influencing physical state, and physical state influencing thought. Dr Joe gives this description of fear:

> *If you have a fearful thought, you start to feel fear. The moment you feel fear, that emotion influences you to think more fearful thoughts, and those thoughts trigger the release of even more chemicals in the brain and body that make you continue to feel more fear.*[13]

Of course, the more you repeat this loop, the more familiar it becomes; this chemical signature of fear (for example) becomes a chemical signature that your body actually craves. Just as you can train your body to rely on nicotine, caffeine or even the dopamine hit that comes from picking up your phone and scrolling, with enough repeated exposure you can train your body to crave the feeling of fear. What happens then is that you unconsciously – and automatically – search for ways to experience that familiar feeling (or thought, or attitude), because this is what you know.

Discovering this was my catalyst for a monumental shift. For so long I'd been telling myself that I wasn't trying hard enough. I'd always go to bed having devoured some kind of self-help tome about 'conquering' anxiety and I'd be filled with hope and determination for the new day. But then I'd wake up bound by the same dilemmas as the day before, and the hope that I'd been so sure of the evening before would tuck itself between the edges of my rib cage, making room for all the parts of me that knew better.

When I read Dr Joe's book, I realised that it wasn't because I hadn't been trying hard enough – in fact, it had nothing really to do with effort at all. These were programs; a way of being that I had remembered to such a degree that it was second nature to me. I longed to feel different, to be different, to think differently and yet, on a chemical level, I longed to feel, think and be exactly the same as the day before.

This means that when we look outside ourselves and see a version of 'normal' in others that doesn't exist in us, we are forgetting that what exists within us is our normal. It may not be comfortable, it may not be what we would consciously choose for ourselves. I mean, obsessing over bowel movements, intrusive thoughts, constantly checking pulse/blood sugar/bathroom locations and relying on rigid rituals are not exactly habits that you would consciously choose for yourself. But that is what has become normal for our body and brain.

How to Stop Doing What You've Always Done

The good news is that you are not confined to this same way of being for the rest of your life. The great thing about habits, and the intelligence of your subconscious mind, is that you can commit new ways of being to memory and, over time, they will become second nature to you. You have been learning new ways of being for your entire life, remembering some, forgetting others – depending on repetition, of course.

Consider that there was once a time when you didn't know how to crawl, let alone walk. You didn't know how to communicate in words, you didn't know how to write your name or dress yourself or look after your own needs. You didn't know how to drive, how use a smart phone. There was a time when you didn't know the thought patterns of *Do they like me? Am I enough?* and the uncertain feelings that come along with those thoughts.

Similarly, there are things you've learnt along the way that you've since forgotten. The layout of your primary school classroom, for example. The lyrics to songs you loved as a pre-teen, or the telephone number of your first boyfriend or girlfriend. These things that were once so familiar to you have now become something you'd struggle to recall in detail. Yet if you were to walk through your primary school classroom now, or hear the opening lines to that song you once loved, they would come flooding back.

The habits that play out in your current experience of anxiety are not the habits that need to continue to play out in your future experience of anxiety. I know that when you are in the thick of anxiety, it can feel like there won't ever be a time when this isn't your reality. In one of the first videos I filmed, where I attempted to leave the house but failed to get out of the driveway, I said: "I can't imagine not being like this. I remember not being like this, but I can't imagine ever going back there, or ever not thinking these thoughts."

When you feel as if you are drowning in dysfunction, it seems impossible that you'll one day be able to breathe more easily. But you will.

And what it takes to get there is not you 'trying harder' or learning how to quiet, suppress or remove the old familiar patterns and pathways. What it takes is a remembering, but of something new this time around.

CHAPTER 10
REMEMBERING SOMETHING NEW

– *The first step in remembering* a new behaviour is – unsurprisingly – to act out the behaviour in the first place. You cannot remember what you do not know, so you need to create a memory to begin with. However, besides being wired for what is familiar and known, human beings have a knack for waiting 'until'. We wait until things get really dire to ask for help, we wait until we can't take it anymore to create change, and we wait until we feel more capable or comfortable before we move in the direction of the things we desire.

I'm no stranger to this waiting. I have waited my entire life for other people to tell me that I'm ready, that I'm okay, that I'm supposed to be doing X Y or Z before I go out and do it (and even then, I still wait).

When it comes to trying new things and creating new habits, we often fall into the trap of thinking that we need to be ready (read: less anxious) before we declare ourselves willing.

I was recently talking to a fellow agoraphobic about his desire to get out and try some exposures. He mentioned that there were a couple of things he wanted to do before he really got out there and bit the bullet. I felt such a tug in my heart when he said this, because I knew what those words meant. I knew that this was his way of waiting 'until'. I knew he didn't feel like he was ready.

Throughout our conversation, he'd talked about all the things he wanted for his life. He talked about the places he thought his journey with anxiety could take him: how he wanted to share his story, and his desire to change the stigma around men's mental health. He talked about the wedding he was planning with his fiancée, and where they hoped to go for their honeymoon. He talked about his newborn nephew and how he wanted to be a positive role model in his life.

He seemed at peace with the idea that his anxiety would play a role in his future; he wanted to take it with him, rather than spend his days standing behind it. But as soon as we started to move the conversation towards the next steps he needed to take – that's when he brought in the waiting. That's when he brought in the 'untils'.

I recognised that this was a safety mechanism. I recognised that this was a way of staying with the familiar, dancing with the known. I recognised myself in all of it, just like I think we probably all can, to some degree.

What I wanted to say to him in that moment was ... do something. Anything. Don't wait.

Because the fact is, the longer he spends waiting, the more he is remembering the same thoughts, the same routines, the same patterns of behaviour that he is so desperate to change. The more familiar he becomes with that same state of being, and the further away he feels from the things he envisions for his life. And the frustrating (but incredible) truth is this: he was only one new behaviour away. That's all it takes – one new behaviour, one small change in routine, then the rhythm he is so familiar with starts to sound very different.

Mark Manson talks about this in his article on motivation[14]. He calls it the 'Do Something Principle', explaining that the nature of motivation (and its tendency to ebb and flow) means that relying on motivation to act as a catalyst for action rarely proves successful. However, doing something, no matter how small or insignificant, creates a chain reaction of both motivation and inspiration, leading to further action.

What this 'something' also does is act as an invitation of sorts. A doorway into a continuing exploration of who we are, what we are capable of, and which direction we should head towards next. We learn things about ourselves that we didn't know, we uncover possibility that we didn't realise was there. As Dr Joe says, "We are all faced with great opportunities disguised as impossible situations."[15] While it can be hard to see the truth in this when you are in the midst of an impossible situation, the concept of 'doing something' makes this truth far easier to access.

Your something might be that you start going for morning walks. Your something might be that you delve into a practice you've always been curious about, like breath work or embroidery or baking. Your something might be that you start a project you've been thinking about, or join a community group that you've held yourself back from, due to fear or uncertainty or worry. Your something might be that you start recording videos of you singing, dancing, painting or talking, and begin uploading them to social media. Or just keep them for yourself. Whatever. But do something. Anything. Do not wait. Do not operate under the assumption that you need to fix what is 'here' before you can find yourself 'there', because that is the same state of being that perpetuates you feeling stuck and unable.

The next step in remembering a behaviour is to repeat it. You need to create repetition, in order to embed this behaviour into the memory of your body and your unconscious mind. When you do this, the behaviour becomes a habit. Slowly but surely, those habits build a structure to your day that looks different to the structure you had three months ago, six months ago, nine months ago. And what's more, the introduction and repetition of any new behaviour inadvertently results in other behaviours to support it.

For example, if your 'something' is that you commit to a practice of walking every morning, it's not just the physical act of walking that you are participating in, but the heading out the door, getting in the car or going down the street, changing your environment from one place to another. You are running into people along the way, maybe coming across a new cafe or store that you might begin to frequent. So you are not only getting used to the pattern of heading out and walking every day, but the pattern of seeing new people, socialising and interacting with the world around you in a way that you otherwise may not have been.

This concept became clear to me when I started a daily practice of home workouts. Buoyed by the idea of 'bouncing back after baby' (an idea I now understand the redundancy of, two babies later), I downloaded a twelve-week fitness program that I could do in the comfort of my own spare room. Because where else was I going to be able to do it?

I was also somewhat soothed by the idea of focusing on something other than my anxiety for a change. It felt nice to have a goal that didn't revolve around exposure or panic or facing my fears in some way or other. So, instead of waking up and lying in bed while running through an exhaustive list of all the reasons I was a shit human being like I usually did, I would get up and deliberately raise my heart rate to uncomfortable levels, sweating and puffing away while my baby rolled around on a play-mat nearby.

After a couple of weeks of this routine, if I had a morning when, for whatever reason, I hadn't been able to do my workout, I felt itchy – I craved it. It felt strange not to do it, as if I had missed something crucial. By the time I finished the program at the end of twelve weeks, I had become used to having that thirty minutes of activity and felt a weird urge to step it up a notch. I found myself – bizarrely – rejoining the local gym, a place I hadn't been to in years.

The first time I went, my hands shook the entire way there. I could barely park my car because of how tense my fingers were around the steering wheel. The second time I went, I ran into a friend I hadn't seen since high school and had an awkward conversation, where I tried to talk about what I'd been up to in a casual, nonchalant way (*Oh, you know, just dealing with crippling panic and an inability to leave the house! How about you?*), while sweating profusely and stumbling over my words. The third time I went, it felt like I'd never really left. I walked in, threw my bag in a locker, and climbed up on the elliptical machine like nothing mattered in the least.

Since the gym became a habit, so too did the drive there. I began to have a period of time (even if only a matter of minutes) where I got used to being in the car again. And the more I repeated that behaviour, the more confident I became with being able to sit in the car without needing to turn around and head home.

When the relationship with my boyfriend finally came to an end, a number of years after it probably should have, the gym became the place I would go to physically release all the pent-up anger and sadness that I'd held within my body. Instead of turning away from uncomfortable emotions, I started to practise actively turning towards them, then letting them lift from my body and my mind.

I also created a habit of daily yoga – waking up and rolling out my yoga mat, regardless of whether I was anxious or tired or cranky or upset – following along with a video on YouTube. This eventually led into not just a love of yoga, but a habit of attending physical yoga classes at a studio twenty minutes from home (when finances and babysitter availability permitted, of course). Once again, this had me spending more time in the car, meaning greater ease in the car and less panic … not to mention becoming comfortable with being in a room among a number of other people for an hour at a time.

This also meant that I became reacquainted with being able to spend a full sixty minutes not thinking about the toilet. It was almost a revelation to me when I found out that I actually could hold my bladder and bowels without having an accident or humiliating myself. Who knew?

When I finally brought myself to join the community mothers' group, which met up weekly, I started to get into the habit of socialising with other mums and babies. This habit was a bit 'shakier', in that it required me to actively participate in conversations or attend the occasional meet-up in a new place (or at someone else's house), to which I some-times opted out. However, I eventually became so familiar with the other mums and the act of being out of my comfort zone that I felt confident enough to go out on my own and join a community playgroup.

This was another regular weekly meeting, with local mums I hadn't yet met, and it was only a matter of time before this hour-long playgroup turned into another hour at the library's story time for kids, and another hour out at a cafe, and a dinner date later that evening with the same mums. Seeing these mums became an important (and familiar) part of my life. Before long, it felt strange to go a few days without some kind of catch-up or playdate or dinner out. I still see them regularly nearly eight years on.

The point is that we have been approaching our anxious behaviours from the wrong angle the whole time. We fixate on these behaviours because of the repetitive nature in which they play out, and we agonise over how we are going to remove them from our experience in order to have a different kind of life. But the 'different' life is not achieved by first stopping the anxious behaviours – and that's the idea that trips us up.

The different life is achieved by *learning and repeating a new set of behaviours*, even when the old behaviours are still very much present. Over time (and quite often, much more quickly than we anticipated) those new behaviours pave the way to a new direction, a new experience, a new way of being that no longer resembles the one we felt so stuck in.

So, where you once started your day by engaging in a tired ricochet between bathroom and bed, you are now waking up, getting dressed, making a coffee and going to work, school, church or wherever. Where you once spent your evenings ruminating and worried, curled up tight and unable to relax, you are now ending the day with a cuppa and a book, or a phone call with a friend, or recording a podcast episode with someone from the other side of the world, heart full and peaceful. Where you once felt caged in a rinse and repeat performance of the same anxious behaviours, thoughts and emotions, you are now moving through life in a way that feels progressive, purposeful and both familiar and unfamiliar at the same time.

It doesn't take a huge leap to create a different experience. It takes little actions, little behaviours, little patterns of being, repeated again and again, until we remember ourselves into a new state of being.

Now I know, this all sounds well and good in theory, but putting it into practice can seem utterly unthinkable, especially if you are someone who has been on the housebound end of the anxiety scale. The idea of doing something, – however small – may be overshadowed by the glaring sense of inability you feel on a daily basis. When panic shows up – and it will – on your morning walk, in your yoga class, or while you're hitting the upload button on your first singing video, the tendency to turn away and walk that old well-trodden path of the known is going to be strong, to say the very least.

The fact is, doing something different to what you usually do is going to cause a reaction in your body. It physically feels as if you are swimming against the tide – I suppose because, in a chemical way, you are. This reaction isn't indicative of a failing on your part (or a sign that you should go back to the old way of being). It's a sign that your body and brain are working as they were designed to. It can also feel mentally exhausting when you are doing something new; this is because you are using all of your attention and energy on thinking and acting in a different way, as opposed to allowing your body to go through the motions of what you've memorised from long ago.

Give yourself space to have that reaction. Know that it's a normal and necessary part of making new neural connections. Know that the very fact that you are able to make new neural connections is an amazing, miraculous, life-changing thing.

Life-changing things should be allowed to feel messy and scary and exhausting

Within that messiness and fear and exhaustion is also exhilaration and freedom and joy. *Life-changing things should be allowed to feel messy and scary and exhausting.*

There's a term within the realm of breath work called 'The Curve of Chaos'. This refers to the sensation experienced during a breath hold, when energy that was previously flowing and expanding is suddenly and decisively contained. It can feel overwhelming and chaotic, both physically and mentally, but it subsides within a few seconds. When I first heard this term, it tugged at something within me. I remember thinking – that's it! That's exactly what it feels like when you start doing different things other than what you know.

Because there is always that initial wave of extreme discomfort – that feeling of *Holy shit, I don't think I can do this*. It seems to rise up into your solar plexus and then hit a peak around your collarbone, and the urge to turn around or give up or go back to what you know drags at your chest, like a weight.

It's here that we can get confused thoughts about what it is we actually want, as in: *I thought I wanted to join this martial arts class, but maybe I actually don't. Or, I thought I was ready to go back to work, but maybe I'm really just not*. We feel this chaotic sensation and we think: *This means that I shouldn't be doing this. This means that I was wrong; I'm not ready, I'm not able*.

But the thing is … if you just stay, if you open to curiosity – to the new and the unknown – the discomfort dissipates. The unknown becomes known. The new becomes old. The things we once thought were utterly unthinkable are now just normal parts of our day that don't require any thought or careful planning or excessive loads of energy.

And you realise, all of a sudden, that you must have remembered something new.

CHAPTER 11

THE WAR AGAINST ANXIETY

*Can we stop trying to fit these shoes not made
for our feet?*

- Ziggy Alberts, from the lyrics of *Keeper*

– The language we use when it comes to anxiety speaks volumes about how we collectively respond to it. We use words and phrases like 'conquer', 'break free', 'tame the anxiety beast'. We talk about fighting anxiety, beating anxiety, finding freedom from anxiety. We utter assurances like "You are not your anxiety!" and "Your anxiety is lying to you! Don't let it win!". We say, "Stay strong. You are stronger than your fears. You are stronger than your worries. *You are stronger than your anxiety.*"

While I understand that the intention behind these words is to convey a sense of solidarity, a verbal offering of strength and resolve in those times when we feel most tired and unsure, I still can't help but feel saddened by our desperation to carve a line between us and one of our most ingrained emotions. Because, while it's true that anxiety is not your defining feature, and it's certainly not the entirety of you, the fact remains that *your anxiety is a part of you.*

Your anxiety isn't lying to you, it isn't an enemy trying to take over your life and destroy your hopes and dreams, and it isn't a separate entity that you need to tame or fight or beat, or an aspect of your being that you need to disown and disembody.

A war waged against anxiety is a war waged against your instincts, against your biology, against your right to access the full spectrum of human experience.

It's not the war against anxiety that feels so awful. It's the war against yourself.

The war we wage against ourselves is a battle that cannot be won. There is nowhere to go when what you are running from is you. There is no place to rest, no way to find peace or ease or a sense of stability. When your entire being is tensed against itself, the sheer exhaustion that eventually overcomes you clouds any hope you had of making it through.

But fighting seems like the only viable option. Because if you aren't actively pushing against all the things you don't want, aren't you just giving in? If you aren't fighting, aren't you surrendering to a life that hurts, a life that is bound by limitations and comfort zones?

A life that doesn't really resemble a life at all?

*It's not the war against anxiety that feels so
awful, it's the war against yourself.*

This is the choice that we seem to be faced with: to fight, to push, to overcome our fears before they overcome us … or to submit to being unhappy, to never moving beyond the things that frighten us. But what we're missing is that it's the fighting that makes everything feel so much harder. It's the fighting that creates more friction – a collision between head and heart. We are trying to hate ourselves into being more capable, trying to divide ourselves into feeling more complete. We throw disgust and disappointment on top of panic and fear, and then we wonder why we feel so utterly overwhelmed.

A journal entry from the time I was housebound reads:

Truly, I'm tired. I'm absolutely exhausted from feeling this fear every second of the goddamned day. I'm tired of fighting it, I'm tired of trying not to fight it, I'm tired of crying and I'm tired of feeling more and more like giving up altogether. If this is what my life is going to continue to be like … I don't want to live.

This refrain was repeated back to me several years later by a young woman, who reached out to me to ask if I had ever felt like giving up. She told me how tired she was from just trying to 'get by' and how she didn't understand why she had to fight so hard. She was angry, she was exhausted. She said, 'I'm starting to think that I'd be better off dead.'

That's a terrifying thought to have: when you are so lost to yourself that you start to think there is nothing left for you here. When you start to wonder if your loved ones would be better off without the 'burden' of your anxiety, when you realise that all the running and pushing and fighting has not got you any closer to where you wanted to be, but instead driven you further away.

These moments are the ones that hurt the most. These moments are the ones that feel the most hopeless, the darkest. You think: *I cannot keep living while feeling like I'm dying. I cannot keep existing while trying not to exist.*

It's not easy to stop fighting though, and there's the rub. We don't want to feel the way we feel. We look around, we see that others don't seem to be having the same extreme reactions to seemingly insignificant things, they don't seem to be struggling like we are, they don't seem to be as disturbed and depleted by the minutiae of daily life. There must be something wrong with us, some way in which we've failed ourselves, and that assumption eats away at our insides like a beetle burrowing deep into the dirt.

And so, of course we fight.

Of course we try to channel the rage at the circumstances we've found ourselves in, in a desperate attempt to change them. But the truth of the matter is that we can't hate our way to where we want to go. We can't keep continuing to fight ourselves at every turn. The cost is too great. We lose parts of ourselves in the battle. We lose the people and the places and the things we hold most dear. We bruise. We splinter. We tense. We harden. We close off our hearts to excitement, to joy, to wonder. Because intertwined within those emotions lies the potential for fear and angst and uncertainty. We don't have the mental (or physical) capacity to feel any worse than we already do.

If we keep exhausting all of our energy on waging this relentless, unwinnable war, we will never really be able to slow down enough to notice the intricacies and complexity in what's here, right now. We will never know a life rich with experience, if we are too busy trying to titrate and control every part of it.

If we keep fighting parts of who we are, we will never truly know ourselves.

And that is the biggest casualty of all.

CHAPTER 12

TO SOFTEN

Night travelers are full of light, and you are, too.

- Rumi, from *Search The Darkness*

– *There will always be emotions* within us that we don't want to feel. There will always be elements of anxiety in our human experience. That is a truth that cannot be disputed, although there was a time when I most definitely would've wanted to argue against it.

I also would have vehemently insisted that there needed to be a distinction made between 'tolerable anxiety' and 'intolerable anxiety'; that I could handle feeling sweaty and nervous if the situation called for it, but not all the time, and not at levels that made it impossible to function day to day.

I think it's important to recognise, however, that both experiences of anxiety – the tolerable and the intolerable – exist on the same spectrum, and that spectrum exists within us. That there is no anxiety if it is not felt, sensed and experienced through our body and brain. Anxiety is not something that we are only going to bump up against if we choose to travel certain paths. I know that for sure, after spending so many years of my life shut inside trying to avoid it, only to feel it every second of every day anyway.

Anxiety is an emotion that belongs to us whether we choose it or not; it will swirl and smoulder within us, regardless of which way we go.

If anxiety is going to show up within us – if we are going to experience it, to feel it, to embody it from time to time, then we may as well allow ourselves to soften towards it. Because when we soften, when we release our held breath and let our shoulders drop and our heart open, we are finally able to access a sense of spaciousness from those emotions that we once felt suffocated by. We can see more, hear more, feel more. When we are not busy fighting ourselves, we are more available to witness everything else that is going on around us: the precious things, the insignificant things, the important things. The little nudges and pokes from the universe that exist to guide us towards whatever it is we are here to do.

When we soften towards our anxiety, we are finally able to unfurl into "the fullness of who we are"[16], as Tara Brach would say.

What's necessary then, is a reunion of sorts. A way of re-establishing the relationship between all of those parts of ourselves that we've been fighting against. One of the most accessible ways towards that, I've found, is to start exploring all the ways in which our anxiety is actually something to be treasured. Something beautiful, something precious.

In *Big Magic*, Liz Gilbert discusses the boring and predictable nature of our fears, stating *"I had fixated upon my fear as if it were the most interesting thing about me, when actually it was the most mundane."*[17] I think there is so much truth to this: we all think that our fears are terrible, hideously unbearable things that make us totally separate from everyone else, and if only others knew how gross and weird our fears were, they would shun us for life. But actually, the opposite is true. Our fears are, more often than not, exactly the same as everybody else's. Dull, vanilla-flavoured fears, mostly traced back to shame and unworthiness and being unlovable.

On the other side of that, however, there is an inherent beauty in the way we respond to our fears; in the way that they can make our heart burst open, in the way we seek out connection and belonging, and the way in which we inevitably end up expressing our deepest, darkest thoughts. There is much of our anxiety that is common and unremarkable; it is repetitive and habitual, a well-rehearsed state of despair. But there is a beauty to be found there, there is a way in which our anxiety eventually calls us to open, to reach out, to get to know ourselves more deeply and intimately than before.

I asked friends on Instagram to tell me one good thing about their anxiety – one thing they appreciate, one thing they've learnt, or one positive thing that their experience of anxiety has led them to. Many answered with more than one good thing. They said things like: "Anxiety has made me realise how resilient I am" and "It caused me to dive deeper into myself." Another said: "It brought me closer to God and strengthened my relationship with my family" and "It helped me to see life beyond myself." There was a lot of talk about anxiety increasing our capacity for empathy, for compassion, for being less judgemental and more accepting of one another and the struggles we all face.

And the answer that came up repeatedly was a variation of: "It's given me the ability to really, truly enjoy life."

This is certainly something that has rung true for me. Everything I do now – from the miraculous to the mundane – feels special in some way. Driving to meet friends for coffee feels precious. Walking my eldest daughter to school is a gift. Sitting here, writing this book, feels nothing less than extraordinary.

And it's not that those things are *without* anxiety. I still experience panic attacks, I still experience overwhelming fear from time to time, and I still sometimes think, *Oh god, what if I accidentally poo?* But I can say, hand on heart, that I love myself through those times. I may still complain about them, I may still sometimes get winded and lost and worried about finding my way through. But I adore the fact that I'm here, having those experiences, living this life. I really and truly appreciate that I'm here, with anxiety. Not without.

So much of our energy and attention is directed towards the presence of anxiety and how it makes us wrong or weak or defective, in some way. But if we zoom out, just a little, we might notice that there is an entire constellation of emotion and knowledge that emanates from that one spark of anxiousness. That we have learnt and discovered and grown in ways completely beyond what we once thought possible, despite and with the presence of anxiety within us.

What continues to be the most valuable lesson for me is knowing that there is no part of me that needs to fight harder, be tougher or otherwise stand up to my anxiety. Claire Weekes, the Australian physician famous for her work with 'nervous suffering', spoke about the futility of trying to cope with anxiety by pushing through, saying: "when the big waves come, we don't stand up against them … we go under them willingly.[18]"

It is not going to help you to stand tense and still in the midst of anxiety; and it's also not going to help you to put your fists up and declare "Come at me!" as if you're readying to fight. What really, truly helps is to dive beneath. To fully immerse yourself in the experience and come out with your hair wet and your skin salty and your eyes crinkled at the edges.

This is when you discover a whole new world below the surface – a world of invigoration, of discovery – a world that at times feels dark and unnerving but at other times is beyond breathtaking.

If you feel called to, you may like to write a list of all the ways in which your anxiety is precious. The ways it has encouraged growth, or perhaps a great wealth of compassion and understanding within. Dive deep beneath the waves and find out what is underneath. You can continue to stand up against the swell of the water and end up being pushed and pulled in every direction, repeatedly shaming yourself for feeling as if you are drowning. Or you can go under willingly, still acknowledging the force of the water but letting yourself really explore it. Moving with it, not against.

Whenever I am feeling at odds with my anxious thoughts, I go through my own list. I remember the places I've travelled to alongside my anxiety, the people I've met, the stories I've written, the ways in which experiencing anxiety has called me towards expressing myself more authentically and honestly. There is beauty here, in our need to survive.

Most of all, I remember that I'm not here to be at war with parts of myself. I'm here to honour, embrace and express each and every part – to embody myself fully. I'm here to dive deep. I'm here to come home.

PART TWO
COURAGE

CHAPTER 13

CULTIVATING COURAGE

Life shrinks or expands according to one's courage.

- Anais Nin, *The Diary of Anais Nin*

- *There is a picture frame* hanging on the wall in our dining room with three photos inside. In the top photo, my sister and I are sitting together on a wall at Hong Kong Disneyland, my eldest daughter – three, at the time – standing between us. The middle photo is a whole family shot: my mum, my dad, my nanna, my sister and brother-in-law, their son, then my daughter and me all standing atop The Peak, a popular tourist attraction thanks to its views over Hong Kong Island. The bottom photo is my dad with the two grandkids; they're playing at one of those 'trick of the eye' photography places where it looks like he is carting them through a village on a rickshaw, but it was really just a painted room.

All of these photos were taken on our last family holiday together. I was two years into my 'recovery' from agoraphobia. By that stage, I had successfully held down a part-time job for a number of months, I was going out of the house with a fair amount of regularity, and my panic attacks had mostly subsided. However, they still visited on the odd occasion, such as if I hadn't had enough sleep, if I was feeling particularly overwhelmed, if the planets were misaligned … you know, all the usual inexplicable reasons that panic attacks pop up. Because of these achievements, I had started tentatively travelling again – a 2-hour road trip here, a 45-minute plane ride to Sydney there – but the 8-hour flight to a whole other country was going to be my biggest undertaking yet.

I had somehow convinced myself that if I could get to Hong Kong and back then I was officially cured. While I'd been dipping my toe in the waters of exposure, there were still days when I'd stay in bed and refuse to go anywhere because my tummy felt a bit 'off'. Attempting to travel to Hong Kong seemed akin to throwing myself into a raging ocean of exposure. No escape. No return. I was going straight into the deep end.

And I was determined to do it. I felt like this was going to be the gateway – the thing that would finally label me 'un-agoraphobic' for good.

Fortuitously (or so I thought), the flight from Melbourne to Hong Kong went without a hitch. I travelled with my daughter, my parents, and my nanna – my sister and her family were going to meet us there, as they were flying in from their home in Sydney. I was incredibly anxious, but managed to maintain a sense of excitement that carried me through. The fact that it was my daughter's first international flight was somewhat of a distraction; managing a three-year-old on an eight-hour flight is nothing if not a serious undertaking.

We arrived in Hong Kong and I felt wonderful. Aside from the random, miniature bouts of panic that burst in my belly like tiny fireworks, I was buoyed by the idea that I was actually doing it. I was overseas. This was a huge accomplishment. (*Holy s**t*, I thought, *I'm actually cured!*)

⇌

When I woke the next morning, however, things did not feel right. What is it about mornings? The excitement had worn off and turned into an all-over sick feeling. I sat on the toilet in the ensuite bathroom, feeling that familiar terror tugging away at my gut. I had stomach cramps and diarrhoea; my tummy always reacted to fear by ejecting experience from my body as quickly as possible.

By the time I made my way down to the hotel's dining room for breakfast, I had also completely lost the ability to speak. The look on my face must have been enough to alert my family to the fact that I was in panic mode; Mum started rubbing my back, Dad tried to distract me with jokes, Nanna kept asking me what was wrong and, when I couldn't answer, repeated softly, "It's alright, sweetheart. You'll be alright."

I felt myself turning inside out. My skin flushed both hot and cold – my neck was on fire. My limbs no longer felt attached to my body; I could feel my head floating up towards the ceiling. *What was I doing here? What had I done? Why, oh god, WHY did I think I would be able to do this?!*

I couldn't go back, and that was my undoing. I was an entire ocean away from home, and home didn't mean anything anyway. I hated the despair I felt, the knowledge that there was nothing I could do to escape it.

I felt the weight of expectation upon me – my family's need to calm me down, my own need to get my shit together. *You're a parent for god's sake,* I raged at myself – and I crumbled beneath it. I was angry, I was terrified, I was desperate. As I looked around, I longed to be allowed to just be. To just be sitting at the breakfast table, eating toast and cereal like everyone else. For the millionth time in only minutes, I asked myself: *What have you done?*

When breakfast was over, I took my daughter up to my parent's hotel room. I sprawled out on their bed, and – finally able to verbalise again – I began to list all the things I was afraid of. I told Mum how awful it felt not to be able to speak, the intensity of the panic in my bones and my organs, the way my skin felt electric and my bowels felt like liquid. I spoke because there was nothing else I could do. And after that, I didn't stop speaking about it.

When my sister met me down in the hotel lobby, I said to her, "Don't let me lose it, okay? If we are out, and it's too much and I can't cope, can you just bring me back here, no questions asked? Don't try and talk me down, don't tell me it'll be okay, just take me back to the hotel as quickly as possible."

"Of course," she said. "No problem."

To her husband, as we sat on the top level of the city tram, on our way to the botanic gardens in the centre of the city, I said, "Hey, I just want you to know I'm trying really hard, but I'm sorry if I ruin the day."

"You aren't ruining anything!" he said. "It's all good, really. Whatever you need is fine. Don't worry about any of it, Lolle."

The more I verbalised my fear, my worry, the less it felt like it was clenching at the back of my skull. I felt normal – not like the situation was normal, because I was having horrendous panic attacks in a totally different country and I still couldn't believe I had actually thought I could do this – but like it wasn't such a big deal to be having these fears. No one else was as bothered by my fears as I was. The world, bizarrely, was still turning.

As the day went on and our exploration around the city continued, I realised that, although I was still terrified and on edge, I had taken some of the sting out of it. I was doing the scary stuff, and it was kind of great, while surreal and dissociative at the same time. Eventually I started cracking jokes, feeling more like myself, able to see the humour in things rather than just unquantifiable terror. I took my nephew and my daughter on a little walk up the mountainside, without focusing on where the closest toilet was. I had a drink with lunch, without worrying that it was somehow going to poison me and make me unbearably sick.

I had various panic attacks throughout the rest of the trip; some minor, some more significant, but none that took away my ability to speak like that first one, and so I kept on speaking. Every time I felt overwhelmed by fear, I spoke about what was overwhelming me; allowing it to have some space outside my body lessened the intensity within my body. Overall, even with the presence of panic, I had a truly wonderful time. In each one of those photos on my dining room wall, I am beaming. A little bit tired, a little bit sweaty with panic, but beaming all the same.

In the end, the trip didn't 'cure' me. I didn't return home magically free from anxiety and panic, and it didn't feel like I had finally farewelled the agoraphobic version of me. In reality, I actually felt closer to my fears than ever – just not in the same way I once had. I didn't feel like I was drowning in my fears but rather swimming freely among them. I felt more in tune with myself, with both the light and the dark inside me. I felt more ready and willing to explore the other things that I was afraid of; I felt a sense of curiosity, as opposed to resistance.

For the first time, I truly understood that courage exists in the exact same place as fear. It was not that I needed to overcome my fears in order to find and embody courage; in fact, I had been a whirlwind of both the entire time.

The fear is where the courage is and, of course,
fear is exactly the place we don't want to go.

Prior to this realisation, the idea of courage had been a somewhat alien concept for me. While my friends and family had insisted that I'd done brave and courageous things – such as seeking help when things got too much, and giving birth to my first daughter throughout a haze of antenatal depression (I remember my sister calling me a 'warrior' at the time, which felt like it couldn't be further from the truth), I personally couldn't see the courage in these acts. These were not things I had done from a place of bravery, these were things I had done while completely and utterly terrified.

Every time, I'd felt like I had my back up against the wall. I had been waiting the entire time for courage to show up, but it never had, so I'd done the only things I could. Courage was not something I had within me. What I had was endless amounts of fear.

But back then, what I had failed to understand was that courage and fear are inextricably linked – you cannot have one without the other. The amount of fear in my body was not indicative of my lack of courage, it was rather an indication of how much courage I truly had available to me at any given moment.

The interesting thing about courage is that we expect its presence will override fear. It's as if we assume that, once we figure out how to conjure this mysterious force, our fears will dissolve into the ether and we will be able to valiantly move forward, free of worry and doubt, instead brimming with bravery, unbounded and strong.

The truth about courage is that it doesn't take away fear and it certainly doesn't override fear – especially when we're sitting around waiting for it to do so. What courage does do, however, is enable us to truly open to our fear; to include it in our movements, then release it once we've done what we wanted to do. Courage allows us to explore fear, to feel fear, to embody all that fear entails. This, I believe, is why we consistently turn away from courage, because it is also inclusive of the things we don't want to feel. The fear is where the courage is, and of course, the fear is exactly the place that we don't want to go.

CHAPTER 14

COURAGE AND YOU

– _Here is something I know_ for certain: you have boundless amounts of courage within you.

The root of the word courage is the Latin word _cor_, which means heart. To have courage means to have heart – and you, my friend, have plenty of that. I know this for sure because I have had the deep pleasure over the years of meeting many folk with anxiety disorders from around the world, and I can tell you that these people are big-hearted, beautiful and loving souls. I have delighted in the friendships that we've cultivated together, and they are connections that I will have for the rest of my life.

Anxious folk feel deeply, they love deeply, they exist in a space of intense emotions because they have within them a truly radical heart. Hear me when I tell you: it is not that you need to have more courage in order to open to the things that scare you, and it is not that you will only find courage once you have 'conquered' your fears.

Courage is not found in conquering fear, courage is found when you make space in your heart for fear to be there. It comes from being truthful about what's really going on inside. We cultivate our courage when we consistently and repeatedly live from our heart space, rather than living from a place of denial.

I think of all the times when I denied myself the reality of what I was experiencing. The times I told myself that my mind was playing tricks on me, that everyone else was doing it – why couldn't I just harden up and get through? I think of all the times that I didn't dare speak my fears, lest they came true, or I felt more shame, or people thought I was weird, or I annoyed someone by being – god forbid – afraid.

And I think of how often this made me feel separate, and as if my body and brain were wrong and strange and always working against me. I think of how often I either didn't do the scary thing, because I didn't have enough courage to 'push through' (and then felt like shit for days on end), or how I did the scary thing while trying to pretend that fear wasn't hot on my skin, and felt accomplished but also utterly depleted (like I'd run a marathon with bricks tied to each ankle). Still coming away from it feeling like shit and wondering – when is this going to get easier?

Conversely, when I finally began to soften to the way my body felt and started speaking openly and honestly about it, making space for all the discomfort to be there – 'doing the scary thing' without fighting myself through – there was a natural progression from that place. Because once you start talking about it, exploring it, letting it land upon your skin while acknowledging that, for whatever reason, it's there – the only thing left to do is move forward alongside of it. You are no longer contracting and trying to escape; instead you are expanding, discovering, taking up space.

It is here, when we allow ourselves to be scared, when we acknowledge that sometimes the world genuinely feels as if it's upside down, instead of insisting that there's nothing wrong … it is here that we feel most honest and true. It is here that we are also able to cultivate connection, belonging and a sense of who we really are. But more about that in coming chapters.

It may seem like what I had done in Hong Kong was, essentially, got my shit together and pushed through my fears. It may seem, from the outside, like I had chosen courage over fear, bravery over anxiety. In reality, though, I'd chosen all of it at once. I hadn't pulled myself together; rather, I'd let myself completely fall apart. I'd let each aspect of me find its place in the experience by telling everyone what it felt like, what I was scared of, what I thought I might need, and the shame I felt at the prospect of 'ruining' the trip. Essentially, I took the hand of both courage and fear, and walked alongside both.

You see, there is a tenderness to courage that we forget about. We are looking for strength, for bravery; we expect a resilience that puffs up our chest and hardens us against the pain and possibility of failure. But true courage brings with it a softness, an honesty (my yoga teacher once said "soft belly, warm heart" and I truly can't think of a better way to describe the embodiment of courage), and we nurture ourselves by leaning into that – by remembering that it is not about closing off to fear and heartache, but by opening up, again and again and again.

This tenderness is sometimes uncomfortable – but not in the same way as trying to remain closed. It feels uncomfortably invigorating, like the sharp, delicious breathlessness that comes from jumping into a cold pool of water on a hot day, or getting to the top of the mountain with your chest heaving and your cheeks red. But you're alive, you're here, you're completely and utterly yourself.

You are courageous.

I know that when you are standing at the precipice of all the things you want, but haven't been able to experience because you are too scared, it doesn't seem like there is a scrap of courage within you. But if I could go to you right now and show you exactly what is in your heart, you would see what I see: the sheer depth of your true and honest ability. Maybe your courage hasn't been burning brightly within your body, but the embers are there – whispering with gentle heat, waiting to be stoked and encouraged. The way you go about that – the stoking, the encouraging – is by inviting each part of yourself to walk forward with you, knowing that with every step you take, even if your hands are shaking – *especially if your hands are shaking* – that's where your courage really sparks.

What it means to be courageous, in my opinion, is to stand at that precipice, acknowledge exactly how scared you are, speak it, and walk forwards with your heart wide open. Don't try and have it all together. Don't try to push through, despite the discomfort. Don't try to challenge the fear. Just walk forward, embodying all of it, exactly as you are. The reason I say 'speak it' in regard to the fear is primarily because, in my experience at least, when we talk about something, we are more open to feeling it. But whether that's you verbally announcing it, writing it out before and after, saying it to a friend or family member, or simply affirming these thoughts to yourself quietly – that's up to you. Whatever you do though, let it land. Let it be there, allow it to have its place.

Time and time again, I have been able to watch from the sidelines as someone has walked themselves through their fear and cultivated their sense of courage. I have spoken to people before and after flights, holidays and trips away, family functions, job interviews and parties. I have listened as they've relayed all their fears to me; all the ways in which things might go wrong, all the worries and the overwhelming doubts. And then I've celebrated with them, as they've come through to the other side.

The common pattern is that none of these people were *without* fear; none of them managed to rid themselves of anxiety sufficiently enough to feel unencumbered and strong before attempting to do something that they found terrifying. All of them, also, had a sense of surprise afterwards – as if they had not expected this from them-selves. And yet, there they were. Sometimes they panicked. Sometimes they didn't. Sometimes things took longer than they anticipated, sometimes they had to go back again the next day and try again.

My favourite thing about being included in these experiences is not that I get to see people do the scary things that they thought they couldn't do, but that I get to see them understand who they really are. Anxious *and* capable. Scared *and* brave. Honest *and* uncertain. All of it, at once. Each time we open to this, we cultivate courage. And that's where life starts to truly expand.

Maybe it's time to stop wishing to be somebody else. Somebody brave, somebody fearless, somebody 'normal' – somebody who doesn't feel like they're going to hurl at the prospect of a social interaction.

Maybe true courage is being exactly who you are at this time, and moving forward as you. If every tiny step, no matter how minuscule or tentative, is taken as authentically and wholly as possible – that is an act of courage. And each of those steps will take you where you want to go. Not as somebody else, but as *you*. The things you perceive to be your fears and shortcomings, the things that hold you back from going after what you want, should not be seen as the enemy of courage, but as the vessels to take you there.

⸺

The things you perceive to be your fears and short-
comings, the things that hold you back from going
after what you want, should not be seen as the enemy
of courage, but as the vessels to take you there.

I want to introduce you to some truths about you. These are heart truths: things that your heart knows to be true, but you've convinced yourself otherwise, for one reason or another. Reminding ourselves of these heart truths is a way to open ourselves to our courage; it's a way of being honest about what's really inside.

These are not the same thing as hard truths. Hard truths are things you may have been saying to yourself for years. Things like: sort your shit out, it's just anxiety, pull yourself together, life is painful, etc. These don't help anyone; in fact, they wound us even more.

Heart truths are the salve for those beliefs we've been hurting ourselves with – the healing balm you can apply when you truly need to know that you are safe. They are:

- *There is nothing you could say or do that would be so humiliating and embarrassing that you'd never be able to go on.*
- *No panic attack is going to be so shameful that you'd be deemed unworthy, unlovable or inhuman.*
- *There is nothing about your anxiety that makes you less deserving of love – that of others, or of your own.*
- *You are beautifully, perfectly, uniquely you – exactly as you are, always.*
- *Regardless of how much fear you feel, or how much you panic, or how impossible things seem sometimes ... you are worthy, always worthy.*

I remind myself of these heart truths often, especially the first one. I can be on the cusp of a panic attack – about to get in the car to go somewhere when that familiar feeling rolls in like a storm cloud – and I stop and tell myself: *There is nothing you could do or say right now that would be so bad that you couldn't live.* And there it is, that tenderness. That opening – a willingness to experience life in all of its messiness, because I know that whatever happens, I'm ultimately going to be okay. The world will keep on turning. That is having heart; that is courage.

If you could move forward through your day knowing these heart truths – knowing how much your heart loves you, knowing that your heart is big enough to hold every single part of your experience – whether or not you're scared or you panic or cry, you would know that nothing really can go so wrong that you'd be permanently bumped off course. You'd know that it doesn't matter how many times you need to try again, because each time you were worthy, regardless of the outcome.

You might like to write your own heart truths, to remind yourself of your access to courage. I took it a step further, and got a sweatshirt with the word 'courageous' stitched onto it. The word is stitched right across my heart space, and it reminds me that courage is always accessible to me, as long as I'm moving from my heart. It reminds me to wear my truth always, because in doing so, I find freedom. In being open and honest about who I am and what I feel, I'm cultivating courage. Always.

CHAPTER 15

FINDING SAFETY IN YOUR BODY

The way out, is in.

- Thich Nhat Hanh, *This Moment is Full of Wonders*

- My relationship with my own body has been strained, over the years.

When I was a child, I had no real concept of my body beyond the fact that I had one, and it worked. My body was simply a vessel for adventure, enabling me to climb trees, make up dance routines, scrabble my way over the large brick fence that surrounded our property, and explore the neighbourhood from sunrise to sunset, occasionally coming home adorned with a scraped knee or two. My body matched my energy – boundless, joyful, imaginative.

As I hit my pubescent years, my relationship with my body changed. I started to become overly aware of how my body fit in with those around me; I began to feel like there were bits I had to hide or change or cast in a certain light in order to be accepted. My body went from being a natural extension of my soul to being something that dictated my self-worth. My arms were too hairy – would boys at school like me? My boobs were too big and my period too early – would friends make fun of me?

I was too much. Too developed, too curvy. Altogether too embarrassing.

As the years passed and I edged my way through high school, I learnt to bend my body to conform to what the standards were. It was the early 2000s, and the collective self-esteem of teenage girls everywhere was about as low as the jeans on our hips. All we spoke about in regard to our bodies was how to burn enough calories to whittle them down to a more appealing size.

I filled my body with nicotine, alcohol, caffeine and hate, seeing how long I could go without actual food and feeling on top of the world if someone happened to mention that I had lost weight. My body and its natural curves and folds was now an irritating stumbling block in the way of achieving all the things that the magazines proclaimed I needed: A Bikini Body, A Revenge Body, A Summer Body. A body that had something to say, rather than something to hide.

Still, throughout this continuing decline in self-love, I maintained a sense of being the one in control of my body. I said jump, and my body would jump. Even my monthly period, which seemed to have a timeline all of its own, I obliterated with the help of contraceptive pills. Rather than taking them as suggested, with a break in between packets, I simply took one active pill after another, skipping my periods altogether.

And then, my body turned on me. Along with the panic attacks and the intolerable anxiety came a complete disconnect between me and my body; no longer did I have any say in my own skin and bones. I said jump, my body said *run*. My body became a place I couldn't inhabit, and as I watched my friends go about their own lives in their own bodies – seemingly with ease – I became more agitated and lost within my own.

It suddenly seemed so alien to me: the concept of being able to go somewhere and do things without your body breaking down. Things like going on road trips, sitting in a car for hours at a time – impossible. Backpacking in faraway countries, exploring cities with a hangover and no real plans – out of the question. Partying at crowded festivals, dancing among a throng of sweaty bodies, taking mind-bending drugs and sharing twenty portaloos between 15,000 people – *how?!*

How were they able to do these things without their bodies protesting? I couldn't even get my body to cooperate enough to get out of bed and walk to the kitchen without becoming overwhelmed by sensation. I think many people must assume that for an agoraphobic, the feeling of being imprisoned in your own home must be the most unsettling and fearful. For me, though, it was being imprisoned within my own body that was the worst part of all.

The degree to which you can interact with the world around you is directly impacted by the degree to which you can interact with your own body. If you can't find any space within yourself to peacefully exist, it's very difficult to take up space outside of yourself. After all, your body is the only true physical home you will ever really have. You have to be able to fully inhabit that home in order to inhabit other spaces, opportunities and hearts. How do you inhabit a body that seems to betray you? How do you find a way to expand, to take up space within your own skin and truly feel at home there, when you're afraid of what's happening inside you?

Perhaps one of the most difficult aspects of anxiety lies within the sheer physicality of it. The survival response may begin in the brain, but anxiety takes only milliseconds to pool in your fingertips, your bowels, your chest, your shoulders. It's there in your breath, your sweat, your heartbeat and your skin. And it is designed to be felt, more so than anything else. When felt in context (before doing something objectively unnerving), it's nowhere near as overwhelming as when felt out of context (for example, when you are simply brushing your teeth on a Tuesday morning).

Unless you've experienced that feeling for an extended period of time with no real reprieve, it's hard to imagine exactly what it feels like. I've often described it as feeling like your body is on fire, while having to walk around pretending that it's not. I've also favoured the phrase 'it feels like I'm crawling out of my skin'. This is ironic, really, because the idea of crawling out of my skin often seemed like a welcoming concept, in comparison to spending the remainder of my life living within it!

What's most frustrating in the way we attempt to deal with anxiety is that even though we've come a long way in exploring the undeniable connection between mind and body, the most common treatments for anxiety are still focused on the mind alone. We get handed pills to alter our brain chemistry, we get referred to a therapist to deal with our thoughts (and, to be clear, I have absolutely no beef with pills or therapy, I am a regular user of both). Yet we don't get any clear nudge towards finding a sense of safety within our own body.

The interesting thing to note about pills and psychotherapy as the frontline treatments for anxiety is that these methods still rely on the body to take part to some degree, in order to access the mind. The body is the gatekeeper to the mind, so to speak. And in the case of anxiety, it's extremely difficult to get past that gatekeeper. For example, in order to take medication, we have to be willing to put up with the side effects that occur within our body: strange sensations that often range anywhere from a clenched jaw to digestive disturbances, vision changes, headaches, muscle cramps, dizziness and nausea, to name just a few. And there's nothing quite like the slew of side effects that you begin to experience, after googling a certain medication before taking it, and reading hundreds upon hundreds of reviews listing all the horrible things that others have experienced from that same medication. (I've done this a truly embarrassing number of times.)

And in order to attend therapy – well, prior to the COVID-19 pandemic and the prominence of telehealth – we actually had to physically attend. My own journey with CBT came to an abrupt end when I was no longer able to drive the six minutes to the therapist's office. I needed therapy to help me with my agoraphobia, yet I couldn't attend therapy *because* of my agoraphobia. It almost would've been funny, had it not been so torturous.

I will admit, during the therapy sessions I was able to attend at least, it wasn't like we ignored the body completely. We would discuss the sensations, feelings and emotions present within my physical being. I would identify those sensations and emotions, rate their 'tolerability' on a scale of 1-10, and go home armed with a plan to expose myself to those sensations again and again until they became more tolerable.

We'd also talk about how those sensations couldn't really hurt me, and I'd almost feel stupid for having been so afraid of them ... until the time came to actually face them and feel them and I'd find myself running in the opposite direction.

The thing was, I understood on a rational level that those sensations couldn't hurt me, and I could rationally argue them away when I wasn't in the thick of them. But then, when my body was alive and electric with discomfort and fear and I was trying everything to stand rigid and put up with it, I ended up crumbling every time. What was rational was completely irrelevant; it didn't matter how much I thought about safety if I didn't truly feel it.

*

The body speaks via sensation. Pain, gurgles, tingling, heat, pangs, twitches, throbbing, 'butterflies' – these are all communications from the body to our conscious mind, vying for our attention at any given moment. As mentioned earlier, the emotions we experience have a physical presence, they are an energy that we can feel within our being, and much of the time, this energy will bring with it a whole host of sensations. Some of these sensations feel pleasant, some feel awful, and some feel so nondescript that they hardly make a ping on our radar of consciousness.

For someone who deals with chronic anxiety and panic attacks, however, every single sensation can feel loud and dominant – as if it were a freight train charging through the body. We are hyper-aware of our inner 'goings on' and extremely quick to attach meaning to all of it. We are desperate to find a sense of safety within our bodies, yet we are the ones who are (oftentimes unconsciously) labelling every sensation as unsafe. A very normal, very minor sensation of food moving through the digestive tract can trigger us to think that our bowels are about to spontaneously evacuate, or the sensation of our pulse quickening can cause us to think we are heading for a heart attack. (I recently had a pins and needles sensation in my forearms and I'm slightly embarrassed to admit that my immediate thought was: *But I'm not ready to die!*)

Instead of trusting our body to do its thing and accepting the sensations that go along with it as just part of the process, we jump on every gurgle or quickening like it's a tolling of the death knell within. I think for a lot of us, if detaching from our physical body was an option, we'd probably do it out of absolute desperation, because nothing else has seemed to work.

If we try to ignore our internal sensations while simultaneously being afraid of them, they tend to become louder and more aggressive in nature. The body is literally screaming, *Listen to me!* and we're standing there with our hands over our metaphorical ears – or, as was often the case for me – popping pills to sedate or shut ourselves up.

For better or worse, it's not totally impossible to get through life by quieting or sedating the body either. I made a significant amount of headway in my early days of agoraphobia exposure by doing exactly that. I would employ every tactic in my bag of tricks to override my body long enough to get myself out of the house. Distraction, affirmations, layer upon layer of clothing, avoidance of stimulants like caffeine or sugar, and always a handful of pills to deal with whatever form of discomfort my body was going to throw my way.

I can vividly remember feeling both totally accomplished and completely crippled by severe stomach cramps when I managed to attend a friend's wedding, by taking eight Imodium pills beforehand – enough so that I could be totally sure that I wouldn't accidentally shit myself. It sounds extreme – doesn't it always? But in my imagination, it was quite possible that I'd become so overwhelmed with panic and anxiety that I'd simply lose the ability to hold on. I could hardly stand up straight the next day, because my stomach was so tight and sore.

And I wasn't sure whether that was a victory or a failure. On the one hand, I was doing the things that I so desperately wanted to be doing – I was out in the world again, hurrah! But on the other hand, was I only going to be able to do them if I medically dulled and sedated myself to the point where I couldn't hear my body? However, I was never able to numb myself to such a degree that I couldn't feel anything at all, and this was where I came unstuck. I could chemically 'cork' myself for a number of days, but sooner or later, I would face a torrential river of discomfort.

Similarly, I could take so many Valium that leaving the house felt almost dreamlike and surreal, but it wouldn't be long before the beating drum of my heart sounded like the stuff of nightmares. If it didn't happen that night, it would certainly happen the following morning – when the after effects of the sedatives I'd taken would leave me physically shaky and emotionally raw.

Wherever you go, there you are, right? No matter how much you try to mentally distance yourself from your physical being, at the end of the day, you just can't escape your own skin and bones.

I think this is where many of us come unstuck – we intuitively recognise that a great divide occurs when we try to override the body and ignore what's going on inside us. We don't feel whole in those moments, we feel at odds with our own being. We know that ignoring the body is not a good idea. We want to be able to comfortably exist within ourselves, and we know that those gentle murmurs from our belly and chest are not supposed to hinder us, but to guide us through life. We hear people say, "listen to your gut!" or "let your intuition guide you". But we aren't sure exactly what that means, because all our time is spent trying not to listen to our gut, or trying to pretend that we can't hear whatever supposed 'lie' our body is telling us.

This can cause such intense frustration that it also divides us from the people around us. They don't seem to understand just how awful it feels within our body – that we are not merely overreacting or being 'too sensitive', but are trying to go about life while pretending that our insides aren't exploding in a spectacular firework display of pure fear, adrenaline and dread, and it is incredibly hard and deeply unsettling to do so.

But … there is hope.

There doesn't have to be this divide – either between you and those around you, or between you and your physical body. There are a (beautiful) multitude of ways in which we can reconnect with ourselves, and it doesn't take overriding, dulling or sedating the body to get there.

I truly believe that when we finally learn to speak the language of the body, we are able to open up to ourselves fully, and also to the world around us. When we lean in, as opposed to repressing or ignoring or turning away, we are no longer stuck in a vicious cycle of fearing sensations and perpetuating further fearful sensations.

When you start to truly listen to – and heed – the messages from your body, you don't need to self-medicate[19], or grit your teeth and muscle through the day. There's no longer an unbridgeable gap between where you are and where you wish to be. Impossibility becomes opportunity, fear becomes curiosity, and it's not only on the tip of your tongue to say 'yes', it's lit up within each and every one of your cells.

Finding safety within your body is also a homecoming, a way of finally finding a space within your flesh, your skin, your bones. And perhaps most beautifully, it becomes a bit of a love affair. You start to learn how to really take care of yourself, how to nurture your physical home, and how to appreciate and honour your needs, wants and desires. If this sounds almost sensual, that's because it is. There is no connection more intimate than the one you will have with you.

Bessel Van Der Kolk, author of *The Body Keeps the Score*, explains:

... the only way to resolve trauma is to get to know yourself and cherish yourself. That is very hard to do as long as your body feels unsafe. Most traumatized people try to get away from their bodies as fast as they can because their bodies stir them up. The body is where the panic is – the fear and the rage. But you need to get to know your rage and your fear and to learn to take care of it.[20]

To add to Bessel's sentiments ... you need to get to know your body.

CHAPTER 16
LEANING INTO SENSATION

– Perhaps one of the easiest ways to attend to and allow sensation is to simply sit in a safe space and notice whatever arises in the physical body.

My version of doing this involves some gentle movement – swaying, rolling my neck around on my shoulders, cat-cow-stretching my spine open and closed; whatever feels accessible and good to me in that moment, generally speaking. The goal in my mind is usually to open my body, bit by bit. And in doing so, to open myself to my own body.

I often think about how many of our movements throughout the day are designed to camouflage and repress: we stifle yawns, we clench our jaw, we hold in farts (because god forbid, we release them in public). We hold ourselves tighter than ever when panicked, existing in a space of constant contraction. We rarely, if ever, allow ourselves to move in order to open; to soften and uncurl, to stretch and release and feel. This exercise is the antidote to that, but it is also a way to familiarise yourself with your internal goings on, without focusing explicitly on that as the end goal.

I would like to note that I very, very rarely do the exercises outlined in self-help books as I read them. It always feels too complicated; it adds a layer of activity that, quite frankly, I didn't sign up for when I settled down to read. Whether you choose to do this exercise now or not is up to you, but I urge you to at least read through it and do it when you've finished reading for the day. I promise, it is startlingly simple but goes a long way towards helping you develop a relationship with yourself.

Noticing Sensations Exercise

Find yourself a comfy space where you can move freely – preferably on the floor or ground, as that is more stable than a bed or couch. A yoga mat might make things easier in terms of comfort, but it's not necessary.

To start this practice, sit on the ground in a comfortable position (I like to prop my butt up on a cushion) and close your eyelids. As you inhale and exhale, you might start to find a gentle movement in your neck, or maybe your shoulders or hips. Maybe you sway backwards and forwards, maybe you find a circular motion, or side to side. Maybe your neck is tired and sore (not surprising, from all that jaw clenching) and it just feels nice to roll it gently around on your shoulders. Allow your body to simply move in the way that it chooses to move, while you breathe in and out.

If you feel called to, start to lift your arms in time with your breath. Lifting them up with the inhale, down with the exhale. Perhaps allowing your hands to float on the way down, and opening them on the way up. Your body will tell you; whatever feels like the best release will be the right movement for you.

As you move, notice the sensations within your physical body. Notice where those sensations occur; whether they drift around, whether there is a heaviness to them, a heat, a tingling. Notice how they might change along with your inhale or exhale. Maybe on some occasions, there are no sensations at all. Just allow your body to move and speak in its own way, and observe what shows up.

Notice how your body acts as a container; it holds every single experience, feeling and thought. It holds your fears, your worries, your assumptions, your beliefs. Your body is not the source of your discomfort, your body is the place in which you are storing your discomfort. And it is retaining that energy as best it can. As you breathe, and as you move, acknowledge just how much you are carrying within this container, and how nice it might feel to make some extra space within. If you'd like to keep moving, you can; if you'd like to wind down your movements, you can begin to do that. You don't need to do anything else, just spend these few moments noticing how much you are carrying within and observing the sensations that may arise throughout your being.

As you do this practice repeatedly, you might find that your movements become greater and more expansive. What starts out as rolling your neck around might become you on all fours, swaying your hips around, or even standing upright and allowing your hands to wrap around your body from one side to another, twisting and twirling your torso. Adriene Mishler of *Yoga With Adriene* calls this 'Knocking On Heaven's Door'[21].

Sometimes it may feel silly, sometimes it may feel hard, sometimes it might produce an emotional response that you weren't expecting. The point of the practice is to become familiar with listening, and the movement is a wonderful way to allow the body to open and speak.

And as you get more in tune with yourself, you may even start to offer compassion and comfort to your body and the sensations inside your physical being. Even if you haven't yet 'accepted' those uncomfortable, panicky sensations, can you still find a way to embrace their presence? To acknowledge that your body is working hard to hold these sensations?

This practice is one that I very much recommend you do every day, if possible. You can do it for two minutes, five minutes, twenty minutes – whatever time and space you have available is fine. Sometimes I do this outside on a yoga mat with my two dogs, Pig and Charlie, hanging out beside me, all of us soaking up the sun and the sounds around us. Sometimes I do it inside with candles and incense and music – the whole gamut. Some days it's enough that I remember at the last minute, and I sit in bed and just rub a hand over my belly while listening to my breath. The point is to spend time consciously tuning in and giving your body the opportunity to move, to speak and to communicate, without trying to repress it or shut it down.

You can find the video of this movement practice on my website iamlaurenrose.com/courageous, as well as short, easy meditations available to download.

CHAPTER 17

COMING HOME THROUGH MOVEMENT

Knowledge is a rumour until it lives in the body.
- The OA (Netflix series)

– In Part One, we explored how emotional energy can become stuck in our physical body when we refuse to truly feel it. The best way I've found to release this stuck energy in a safe, healthy and constructive way is with physical movement. Yep – I am talking about exercise, but maybe not in the way we often talk about exercise.

I think there is a very particular difference between exercise in relation to fitness (or weight loss) and exercise in relation to releasing all the things we've been keeping locked inside our physical being. The former is about working and/or changing the body, and the latter is about *knowing* the body.

There are so many recommendations to use physical activity as a way of relieving anxiety and for good reason, because it helps. But we forget that a goal of moving our physical body should also be so that we can live more authentically and freely within it.

I don't ever remember being taught in school that physical movement has a language all of its own, and that it's nothing to do with the way you look, nor the healthy food pyramid. Physical movement is a way to remember who you are, to get to know yourself deeply, and to give voice to what cannot be intellectualised or expressed in words.

In her book *The Joy of Movement*, Kelly McGonigal talks about proprioception, also known as kinaesthesia, which is the way we are able to sense our physical body and its movements[22]. To give you an example, if I asked you to close your eyes and touch your nose, you'd be able to do so even though you cannot see yourself doing it. This is proprioception at work. Your brain knows where your hand is, because all the muscles in your body are constantly communicating with your brain via signals and sensation.

These signals relay essential data to your brain, including a perception of who you are based on your body. You might have a sense of whether you are fast or slow, strong or weak, based on the data your brain has received from your body over time. To give you another example, I've always been a really crap dancer. As much as I enjoy dancing, I have a sense of myself when I'm moving to a beat – or, to be more accurate, I have a sense that I'm not in time with the beat. Even though I'm not watching myself dance, I'm able to perceive that I'm not the greatest dancer because I can sense the awkwardness of my physical movements when I'm dancing. (Now I'm thinking about it, perhaps half the reason why I 'can't' dance is because I'm too busy perceiving how I look while I'm doing it.)

It makes sense then, that all the time us anxious folk have spent avoiding the shit that scares us, running away from internal sensations because they feel like the end of the world, and losing sleep over all the worst-case scenarios, we have decided a 'truth' about ourselves based on this information: we are incapable; we are scared; there is something wrong with us.

The way we move our body has taught us that we always feel unsafe.

Think about the things you've decided to be true about yourself, based on the way you've been moving through the world (or rather, *not* moving through the world, as was the case with me). These may have seemed like facts – most likely, because you have been physically living them out. But these facts are simply a reflection of the signals from your body and how you've interpreted those signals to mean about who you are.

For me, the things I'd decided were true were things like 'my anxiety is always at its worst in the morning', which lead me to 'I can't do anything until I've had a few hours to regulate myself and settle my thoughts'. I also maintained that I was 'a really sensitive person who cries a lot' and 'I'm not good at adjusting to change'. I also probably would've told you that I can't sit in the car for a long period of time, purely based on the notion that I was scared of doing so and actively avoided it. As it turns out, these weren't truths at all, these were just assumptions based on data from my physical body to my mind.

As McGonigal discusses in *The Joy of Movement*, physical movement gives us a way to change our minds about those 'truths', to discover that we are, in fact, capable and whole[23]. And no matter how many times we may have spoken and affirmed this to ourselves, until we have a felt sense that this is true, it's just a rumour – just as the quote at the beginning of this chapter said.

***

The way we move our body has taught
us that we always feel unsafe.

***

I discovered this 'felt sense' for myself during my first yin yoga class. For the years prior, I had used exercise as a way to mould and shape my body into submission, and even though I'd noticed that much of the physical exercise I'd done since dealing with anxiety had given me that glorious rush of endorphins and made me feel good, I still hadn't quite learnt that there was more to it than runner's high and getting 'shredded'. It was still a case of: *I will exercise so that I look better, and that will inevitably give me more confidence, so I will panic less.* AKA, I will be someone 'different' and therefore 'better'.

There was so much about yin yoga that was polar opposite to every other form of exercise I'd ever done. For example, we were encouraged to wear whatever felt comfortable – whether that was track pants and a cosy jumper, or leggings and long socks and extra layers. The poses, mostly floor-based, are held for a long period of time. I was shocked when the teacher said we'd only be doing five different poses for the duration of the sixty-minute class. Just how long were we going to be holding those poses?! (three to seven minutes, as it turned out).

The class finished with what seemed to be a nap (savasana), for which we were encouraged to use blankets and pillows, in order to feel as relaxed as possible.

Never before had I spent an exercise class so deliberately and intently listening to my body; because of this, it was during yin that I finally came to feel my body, to meet it, to hear it. I have had many experiences since, during yin classes, where I literally hear my body speaking to me, which sounds almost insane, I know. But it is honestly the most wonderful and intimate experience, regardless of how genuinely nuts it makes me seem. The title for this book, in fact, came to me during a yin class. I first heard it as 'taking ages' which, given the structure of the class, wasn't a surprising message. But as I listened more, I realised it was 'courageous' rather than 'taking ages'. C-o-u-r-a-g-e-o-u-s, the word stretched out in my body and mind. Here you are, I heard. Courageous.

On a physical (and less crazy-sounding) level, the long, static holding of poses during yin yoga allows the stretch to access the fascia of the body. Fascia is the connective tissue that envelopes our muscles, tendons, organs and bones – it encompasses everything within our physical being and is part of what literally shapes us. There is an entire school of thought that suggests we hold trauma and memories within our fascia. Again, you might remember the words of Candace Pert discussing how emotion becomes 'lodged' in the body.

Fascia is informed by our muscles and nervous system. It contains sensory receptors which detect changes within the body; so if our muscles are constantly contracting and our nervous system firing on fight or flight, the fascia remembers this and responds accordingly. It makes sense then, that for a body which is forever trying to suppress sensation and is tight with tension and fear, the fascia would remember this state more clearly than a state of relaxation and calm.

It's also worth noting that fascia responds to resistance with more resistance, much like the way we respond to anxiety with – you know – more anxiety. The best way to stretch and release fascia is to ease into it, rather than muscle your way in. It's for this reason that I think what we do in yin yoga truly mirrors what happens in our bodies when we drop resistance and stop trying to fight our anxiety. Instead of tensing up against our fear and maintaining a repetitive hardening, it's a softening, a continuous invitation to open, again and again, a little more each time.

Of course, if yin isn't your thing, then it isn't your thing, and that's perfectly okay. Different strokes for different folks, and all that. But there will be an exercise that lights you up inside, so that you truly recognise yourself in there. There will be an exercise that brings you home. Your job is to find what that exercise is.

Restorative practices such as tai chi, qi gong and gentle swimming are known to be wonderful for balancing the nervous system and encouraging mental and physical opening in a moderate way, just as more physically demanding activities such as running, weight-lifting and cycling are known to be wonderful for stimulating endorphins (those feel-good chemicals), encouraging healthy brain cell growth and building a sense of resilience and adaptability.

Whatever exercise appeals to you, you will find that engaging in it gives your body a space in which to move, to feel – which, remember, is how the body speaks – and to release all the pent-up shit that we store for the purpose of trying not to feel it. Physical exercise is your place to move all of that contracted, panicked energy through and out; it's your place to finally allow those sensations to dance and simmer around your body until they dissolve into nothingness.

There are a million ways to move your body, especially when you expand your definition of 'moving your body' beyond the realm of fitness and exercise. You might choose to take up a water-based practice such as kayaking, stand-up paddleboarding, surfing or simply immersing yourself in salty water and letting your body drift and float as you choose. You might start hiking – exploring the trails and mountains, discovering yourself among the trees and the rocks and the wildlife. You might choose to take up a creative style of movement – I was surprised at just how physically demanding wheel-throwing was when I took a pottery class earlier this year, and I marvelled at how changing the amount of pressure in my forearms translated to patterns and shapes in the clay.

Whether it's indoor (or outdoor) rock climbing, bouldering, dancing, taking up golf or baseball or softball or netball or any of the other ball sports, gardening, cycling, Pilates, skateboarding, or jumping on a trampoline for the pure joy of it. Whatever you choose to do in order to find movement, if you do so with the intention of getting to know yourself, you will find that the heaviness you have been carrying so tightly within you will start to release. And you'll discover things about yourself that you thought were lost to you completely.

The language of your body and the way you express yourself doesn't need to follow a set guide. Similarly, it may change from day to day, year to year. Where I once found myself happiest in the weights room, attempting to master the proper squat form, I now find myself feeling both rested and deeply alive on the yoga mat in my lounge room, mastering the art of moving slowly and intuitively along with my breath.

The point is, in my opinion anyway, to find a place in which your body can move and speak, a place where you can really feel all the sensations that wish to be felt in an environment that is joyful and releasing to you. It's very hard to find safety in your body until you begin to start using your body – it is only then that you can start to slowly inhabit yourself again.

This is the paradox: we have been desperately trying to find safety in order to unfurl back into ourselves, yet it is in the unfurling that we *create* safety. It is in moving our body and tuning into our body that we find those sensations are no longer frightening or alarming, and we give ourselves permission to truly feel.

CHAPTER 18

CONNECTION

~

We are all just walking each other home.

- Ram Dass and Mirabai Bush, *Walking Each Other Home*

– Within each of us is a strong desire for connection; we are wired to seek it out. Connection allows us to feel at home in the world around us. We are better able to find meaning and purpose, to self-regulate, and to handle both external and internal stress when we have a strong support network around us and feel that we really belong.

We've always had this need for belonging. For our ancestors, our survival as a species depended on our belonging to the tribe, and our ability to develop and maintain relationships. Social rejection back then was a matter of life or death, and though it's not that vital today, we've still evolved to crave acceptance and fear rejection.

An article published by the Proceedings of the National Academy of Sciences (PNAS), showed that we actually experience social rejection in the same way as we experience physical pain[24]. It seems that being excluded is as much a punch to the chest as it is a hit to the ego.

The caveat with belonging, however, is that it needs to be real. It needs to feel genuine and authentic, in order to really make a difference. That is why you can be in a room full of people and still feel completely alone, or have a busy social life and still feel as if you don't have anyone to turn to in times of distress. In order to develop and nurture authentic and genuine relationships, you need to be authentic and genuine. You need to allow yourself to be seen – which is incredibly hard to do when it comes to panic and anxiety.

So much of anxiety and panic is a closing off, a retracting, a pulling away. Yet our need for authentic relationships requires us to open. When you are working so hard to hide from yourself, how can you possibly allow somebody else to really see you? How can you allow someone to know you – and all those parts of you that you are so deeply ashamed of?

This is where we feel torn, where our needs conflict with our desires.

We have an inherent need to connect, to be heard and held and seen, coupled with a deepseated desire to avoid shame and judgement. We assume that all of those aspects of ourselves that we find undesirable and uncomfortable are going to be just as undesirable and uncomfortable for everyone else. There have been countless times when I've tried to hide my panic from others in the moment, or times when I've made up some excuse as to why I couldn't attend a social event or meet up for a coffee, rather than just saying, "I feel too anxious today."

We wind ourselves so tightly in this secrecy and shame about our condition that we no longer have any space to breathe, never mind belong. And even though we may consciously know that we won't be cast aside for feeling anxious and afraid, we still keep ourselves at arm's length from everyone else – a kind of self-enforced separation – in order to avoid feeling separate. And it's exhausting – this obsessing, this pulling away from everyone else and from ourselves at the same time.

What often ends up happening is that we only show up as half of ourselves – a strange, censored version that doesn't truly represent who we are, and leaves us awake at 3am questioning every single thing we said, worrying about how we came across.

Or we just don't show up at all. We cancel at the last minute, then feel embarrassed for being so flaky and unreliable. As all of our failings as normal, functioning members of society keep accruing – even though we're the only ones keeping score – we become unequivocally convinced that we don't belong in this world, and we shrink even further away.

⌁

There came a point where I grew tired of shrinking. Partly out of boredom, mostly out of loneliness, I created a blog under the pseudonym 'anxietymamma'. I claimed this was a play on words because I was a mother and I had anxiety (creative, I know) but really it was a way for me to speak about my fears without connecting myself to them in any real way.

I used the blog as a space to talk candidly about my mental health, alongside benign, Pinterest-able topics like 'what's in my make-up bag' and 'vegan lemon slice'. The blog was followed by an Instagram account and then a YouTube channel – which was considerably less anonymous, given that I uploaded videos of myself. However, as far as I could tell, no one in my real life knew about it.

Because when it came to said 'real life', I found it extremely difficult to broach the subject of my anxiety issues. Although my immediate family and close friends knew about my anxiety, at the crux of it there was still an assortment of worries and obsessions that I was too embarrassed to openly discuss. Most notably, the fear of not making it to the bathroom in time – that was the giant elephant in the room that I couldn't even make eye contact with, let alone talk about. Looking back, I'm sure that my obsession with the toilet was obvious to everyone, given how long I spent in the bathroom, going to the bathroom or trying to find a bathroom. But to talk about it meant to admit it, and that wasn't something I was willing to do.

⚡

It felt as if I was forever trying to outrun that feeling of shame.

⚡

This was partly due to an extreme, irrational fear that if I spoke about it out loud, it would somehow make it more likely to come true. As if just saying the words, *I'm frightened that I'm going to shit myself,* would somehow affirm it into being. More than that though, it was the pervading sense of shame that kept me from broaching the topic with anyone – even my closest friends who knew me inside and out. I was deeply, deeply ashamed, not just at the prospect of soiling myself in front of people, but at the fact that I was afraid of it in the first place.

The fear of losing control of bowel function didn't seem to be something that anybody else was afraid of. Nobody else I knew was torturing themselves day and night with visions of not making it to the bathroom in time; nor did they have panic attacks when they left the house, or break into an unbearable sweat while standing in line at the pharmacy, all because their tummy happened to gurgle.

It felt as if I was forever trying to outrun that feeling of shame; trying to cover up my panic attacks in public, trying to avoid shitting myself, and doing everything I could to prevent discussing it with people who cared about me. If I talked about it, it would catch up and I'd lose myself to the humiliation of it all.

However, in the online world, admitting to my fears was far easier. I suppose that was because it felt as if I had some distance from my fears; they weren't all over me, rather, they were abstract ideas. Online, I could remove those uncomfortable feelings from myself and arrange them into words in a manner that made sense. I could create some order out of the chaos in my body and brain, and it helped.

What arguably helped the most was that, through my blog and my videos, I began to connect with other people who were going through similar struggles to mine. I found fellow agoraphobics – incredibly hard to find in the wild, as you can imagine – and anxious folk like myself, who would message me and share their own story with me. We'd email back and forth, sharing our various accomplishments and commiserating with one another on the harder days.

The video I uploaded to YouTube titled, *Let's Talk Toilet Anxiety*, ended up being the most viewed video on my channel (and still is to this day), with the most frequent comment being along the lines of: "Oh my god, I thought it was only me!" These interactions paved the way for me to finally become comfortable talking about my anxiety, both online and in person. Because in truth, it wasn't so much that I craved distance from my disorder but connection. I needed to know that it wasn't just me – that there was somebody else out there who felt the same way I did.

I had initially thought that writing a blog and creating social media accounts was just a means of staying relevant and showing up in a way that I could control. But in retrospect, I can see that it was more of a searching. Each post was me saying, "Is anybody out there?" during a time when I felt most alone. I longed to feel safe and secure. To finally feel held.

I'd spent so much of my energy hating myself; trying to be better, less anxious, more likeable. I was exhausted and desperate for someone to finally tell me that it was okay to be who I was.

I'd

The real shame in holding ourselves back from connecting with others is that we are not only robbing ourselves of the chance to feel seen and held, but we are robbing others of an opportunity to feel seen and held too. There are millions of people out there who are desperate to show up as they really are but are terrified of doing so, in case they don't 'fit in'. By refusing to be honest about how we feel, we perpetuate a collective state of unease which ultimately creates more anxiety, more shame, more secrecy. More souls who don't realise that they really do belong.

We need to remember that it's not our being perfect human beings that qualifies our belonging; it's not the absence of anxiety or quirks or messiness. It's in these so-called 'undesirable traits' that we most readily recognise ourselves in one another; we see a truth that we can connect to and understand. It may not be easy to shine a light on those aspects of ourselves that we are so desperate to hide. But when we do finally allow our more vulnerable side to come to the party – as terrifying as it feels to do so – we find that some of the heaviness lifts. We realise that we have many hands to hold and hearts to rest within.

Michael[25], one of my first podcast guests, shared this:

Really speaking openly [about my anxiety] ... the amount of people that reached out to me being like, "Oh my god, I'm so glad you said this, I feel this way too, I didn't know what to call it ... " or "I've experienced this in the past" ... people I had no idea, you know, would not have suspected ... I feel pounds lighter than I did before sharing that.

CHAPTER 19

FINDING BELONGING

– So how do we strengthen our sense of belonging when it feels impossible? How do we open out, when our fear tells us to contract?

One of the most basic places to start, though it may sound remarkably insignificant, is by making eye contact. Looking one another in the eye seems straightforward enough, but in a world where we spend every second of our idle moments staring at a device in our hand, meeting another's gaze is something that we very rarely do. And in saying that, for those of us who experience social anxiety, staring at a phone screen to avoid looking people in the eye is often less of a way to pass time and more of a necessary coping strategy. To look somebody directly in the eye feels like it's somehow exposing you more than it is them. You can't hide when you are eye to eye with another human, and that's an incredibly vulnerable thing.

Something helpful to remember about eye contact, though – especially for us anxious folk – is that it can serve as an anchor, a way of grounding, when you feel as if your consciousness is floating away. As children, we constantly look to our caregivers, to make sure that they are nearby, they are watching, we are safe. As adults, however, we shy away from doing it. I guess that's because looking for reassurance is another way of showing vulnerability. (And we'll be damned if we're going to do that, right?)

When I first started doing my version of exposure therapy, one thing I found to be extremely helpful was making eye contact with those around me. Although the irony wasn't lost on me, for someone so terrified of going out in public in case I made a dick of myself and people saw me, the thing that soothed me most was making sure that people saw me. The reason it helped me so much was that it immediately brought me back down to earth and connected me with the rest of the world. I'd be emotionally running away with every single alarming and uncomfortable sensation, rushing through the motions, trying to beat the panic, drowning under the weight of my own awareness, and then I'd make eye contact with another human and remember: *There is an entire world moving around me.*

There are people going about their day, with their own trials and tribulations: someone is late to pick their kids up from school and is trying to figure out what to make for dinner; someone else is just coming from an appointment with their acupuncturist for a chronic back injury; someone else is thinking about the crappy date they went on four nights ago and hoping that the next isn't as bad. I'm not alone, I'm not standing out, I'm not especially different or unique, I'm just here among all these other human beings, and I'm only relevant to them for this split second in which we make eye contact. I'd always smile – the most genuine smile I could manage, even if my back was dripping with sweat – and for just a moment, I'd feel relieved of my own stupid self-importance.

It's also been suggested that eye contact can stimulate mirror neurons, which help us to feel internally what we are experiencing externally. So if someone were to make eye contact with you and smile, neurons start to fire in your brain – the same neurons that would fire if you were smiling at someone. When we make eye contact, our capacity for empathy seems to increase; that is, we feel what the other is feeling. (To see a beautiful video which really highlights this, search YouTube for *Look Beyond Borders – 4 Minutes Experiment*).

If you find making eye contact is uncomfortable – as I often do – that's okay. Practise. We are genuinely so out of the habit of really looking at one another that it's probably going to feel uncomfortable before it starts to feel like second nature, but it will eventually become easier. And honestly, I think taking the time to look at and really see each other is a skill worth practising. I think of my daughters growing up in a world where, instead of keeping their eyes cast downwards at a screen, staying locked in worry about their inner world, they can look up and at those around them and realise that they are held, they are loved, they are as much a part of this big beautiful world as everyone else. Do not underestimate the power of meeting another's eye, and the message that we can convey with that one simple act.

Another way of building belonging is to "be the longing", as described by poet and writer Toko-Pa Turner. In her truly beautiful book, *Belonging*, Toko-Pa says:

Where you long for the friend who calls only to find out if you're well, be that caller for another. Where you long for eloquent prayers to be made of everyday things, let your own clumsy words bless your meals out loud. Where you wish for ritual under the moons, be the one who holds the heartbeat of gathering. Where you ache to be recognized, allow yourself to be seen. Where you long to be known, sit next to someone and listen for insight into what they love. Where you wish you felt necessary, give those gifts away.[26]

In other words, be for others what you wish someone would be for you. This doesn't have to be a life-changing act of kindness; it can be something small and simple, like sending a text message to check in or donating something you no longer need to a service or person needing it.

During the pandemic, we all experienced the heartache of multiple lockdowns and intense social restrictions; the collective fear, uncertainty and struggle was palpable. But one of the most significant things I noticed during that time was how many people took it upon themselves to be of service in whatever way they could. People put baskets outside their houses with supplies, free to take if you needed anything. Fences were painted with uplifting quotes and signs. Somebody would put a call out on a local Facebook page for something they needed, and hundreds of people would respond offering their help. Someone in my neigh-bourhood put out a tray of sunflower seedlings for people to take home and plant in their own garden, to brighten what had become really dark days.

In a time where none of us knew what was going to happen next and how long it would be until we'd be reunited with family and friends, complete strangers showed up for one another and banded together to ensure that everybody had what they needed. We realised that we could do *some-thing*, and that was to care for one another.

When it comes to anxiety, we tend to become convinced that we have nothing of value to offer. If your anxiety manifests in a way that leaves you housebound, you might wonder what it is you could possibly offer to somebody else when you can't even leave the house. There is always some-thing that you can do; you may just have to be creative in your offering of it. Is there something that you could send out into the world? One thing that I know for certain is that you could offer your experience. Your knowing.

The poet Sean Thomas Dougherty said, "Why bother? Because right now, there is someone out there with a wound in the exact shape of your words.[27]"

This reminds me that even when it feels like I'm exposing myself by sharing vulnerable things – such as my incessant fear of not being able to make it to a toilet in time – there is somebody out there, maybe just one person, who may benefit from my sharing it. There is someone out there who is experiencing something similar to what you've experienced, and they are desperately searching for a sign that there is a path ahead, if only they keep going. You may feel as if your struggles count you out from being able to contribute, but the opposite is true. Your struggles often imprint you with a wealth of wisdom, and in sharing that wisdom you might just ease someone else's struggle.

While I didn't realise it at the time, when I was housebound the absence of the wild, natural world was a big part of why I felt so engulfed in my problems. It was only when I started taking myself out for 'exposure walks' that I noticed how being outside among the trees, the breeze and the soil actually lifted some of the weight from my body. I would wrap layer upon layer of clothing around myself, pack a bag full of 'emergency' items that I imagined I might need (but never used), put my headphones in, buckle my daughter into her pram and off we'd go, down to the river near my house.

In the winter, there was something about the chill in the air that would pull the worry from my chest; I'd feel alive and reassuringly present in the world. As the days got warmer and summer rolled around, I found that the soft heat of the morning would soak into my skin and I'd feel my muscles relax, the impulse to rush (to avoid discomfort) would give way, and I'd finally be able to slow down.

Outside, I would feel creative, inspired, hopeful – my mind alive with plans. At home, in the same unchanged environment, I'd find myself reliving over and over again the same fears and anxieties, a repetitive dance with despair. Outside, I felt anchored and connected to the whole; inside I felt tethered, unable to escape myself.

It's a strange thing, how much time we've spent ignoring the power of nature when it comes to regulating ourselves. I don't remember any of my therapists or doctors recommending that I take myself outside into nature, in order to calm my nerves. Not one professional said to me: "Do you know what will help? A big lungful of fresh, cold air and a walk in the wild. Here's a prescription for a long afternoon hike; repeat three times weekly or as required." Of course, I'm being a bit over the top there – and to be honest, when I was at my absolute lowest, I probably would've bemoaned my inability to actually get anywhere in order to gulp that fresh air and walk in that wild. But still, it has to be said that there is so much money and time spent trying to chase wellness in the form of a supplement or a fitness trend or a new type of body therapy, yet we forget one of the most wondrous and expansive therapies is available to us always, for no cost at all.

Immersing ourselves in nature reduces nervous system arousal, lowers blood pressure, improves cognitive and immune function, as well as our mood, physical activity levels and sleep. But much more than that – nature connects us more deeply to ourselves and to the world around us. Nature helps us to realise that we are here. We belong.

There is a wildness within us that is at home in nature. Ruth Allen talks about this in her book, *Grounded*. She explains that each of us have this inner wildness that is always trying to emerge, yet in our day-to-day life we often try to suppress it. However, put us out among the trees and the wildlife and there is an instant sense of ease, as if our inner wild can breathe freely when connected with the natural world[28].

I've experienced this so many times when I've been out on a hike or swimming in the waves. I feel more myself than ever. I'm not afraid or unsure or fearful of judgement, because everything that is in me is also there in the water, the air, the leaves, the dirt. The heartbeat of the natural world is always alive within us and we are alive within nature.

Nature doesn't care how you show up.

Wherever it is available to you, immerse yourself in nature. Whether it's a walk in a local park, watching the sunset/sunrise each day, a swim in salty water, a day trip to the nearest and biggest hill you can climb, or just sitting outside and feeling the breeze touch your skin … go and find your belonging in nature. If you can find somewhere to mindfully explore, somewhere you can lose yourself in the landscape and find yourself in the smallest of details, then go. But, please god, don't make the mistake of waiting until you're 'ready' to get out there and submerge yourself in the natural world. For example, if your anxiety happened to be particularly bad that day so you are tempted to think: *I'll go for that walk or swim tomorrow, when I feel better.*

So many times, I held myself back from really exploring the world around me, especially if it was somewhere unfamiliar and I wasn't certain that there would be a public toilet nearby. I'd sit in my room, procrastinating, becoming more and more convinced of my own inability. Conversely, the times that I made it outside among the trees, I didn't even care where the toilet was. I wondered what took me so long!

Nature doesn't care how you show up. There is a place for you in nature, whether your hands are trembling, your stomach is swirling or your chest is tight. The wild will open its arms to you, no matter who or how or what you are. And maybe, the wild is where you will find yourself. Out among the trees and the grass, the hills and the breeze. Maybe the wild is where we have always belonged.

CHAPTER 20
NURTURING RELATIONSHIPS

– A _theme that recurs again_ and again in the anxiety realm is how much we worry (surprise, surprise!) about how our anxiety impacts on our ability to sustain nurturing, loving relationships – not just romantic relationships, but relationships with family, friends and people we need to interact with on a daily basis. So many anxious folk that I've spoken to over the years have mentioned how they feel that their anxiety is a burden on their loved ones, which leads them to either suppress it or deny it, or they are smothered by a sense of letting everyone down, because they are _unable_ to suppress or deny it.

Maintaining a relationship with anyone else is difficult when your relationship with yourself is frayed, hence the adage: _You must love yourself before you can love another._ In saying that, given our innate need for connection, we need nurturing relationships like a fish needs water. We need to feel held and loved.

So the important questions are: How do we ensure that we are showing up in our relationships inasmuch as we can?

How do we prevent our anxieties from feeling burdensome for our loved ones?

I'm not an expert in this area by any means. But after many years spent navigating my anxiety while also being a parent, a partner, a daughter, a sister, a friend, an aunty and so on, I've got some thoughts on the matter. I also asked my friends and family for their thoughts on this, because I figured it was important to get some perspectives other than my own.

The words that came up, again and again, were honesty, reciprocity and communication. It seems that both parties want to be able to speak honestly, without fear of judgement. We each need space to speak and feel heard; sometimes that means acknowledging that our actions and behaviours are going to have an effect on the people we love, so we need to allow space for that to be the truth without getting defensive or victimised by it.

Additionally, we each need to feel that what we give to the relationship is returned, in some form or other. This is something that used to worry me a lot, because I felt that due to my anxiety, I wasn't able to reciprocate. For example, when I was housebound, I wondered how my friends could still stand by me when I stopped attending any of the special events in their lives. If I denied every invitation and every call for interaction because I was afraid then surely, they would give up on me at some point?

What I learnt is this: there are more ways than one to show up for your loved ones, if you can't physically be there. In an age where text messages are the norm, a phone call can mean everything. Or a letter. A meaningful gift. Making the effort to meet a friend when you can; and if that means at your house in your PJs, then so be it. I think all we really want at the end of the day is to feel that we are cared for – that the people we love, love us just as much.

If there are relationships that do fade away, even with your best efforts, they were not for you. That was the hardest pill for me to swallow; as a people pleaser, I am always horrified by the idea that someone just might not like me, or that I won't be able to fulfil everyone's needs. The important thing to know is that it's not, and never was, about your anxiety.

Relationships are not static things; they ebb and flow, they grow and change. Who and what was once right for you may not be right for you next week or next year; the healthiest thing we can do is to appreciate those people for what they brought into our lives, hope that we brought something into theirs, and with respect – let go.

When you begin to open up to the world around you, something incredibly magical happens: you start to find the people and places in which you feel most at home. You start to find community. When the prospect of connecting with one or two people seems overwhelming, the idea of connecting with a community of people can feel virtually impossible. But actually, it's having a common link with people that allows you to feel more able to show up exactly as you are. It's within community that we seem to catapult our way towards healing – we discover a resolve that wasn't there before.

Community is where we truly understand that we aren't walking through this life as just one.

As much as I curse Instagram for being a black hole for my attention and time, I am also deeply grateful that it has allowed me to connect so genuinely with other anxious folk. If it weren't for posting those little squares whenever I did an exposure (or had a thought I needed to get off my chest), I would never have found myself nestled among such a beautiful and encouraging community. These were people who really got it – they understood why it was so difficult for me to get out of the house or drive down the street, and they were there for all of it: the uncomfortable and messy bits, and the triumphant and happy bits. And because they understood and they were there with me (albeit not in person), I became more willing to be there with myself too. I became more willing to try, to actually attempt to spend time in discomfort, because I knew that I wasn't alone.

Community is where we truly understand that we aren't walking through this life as just one; instead we are all leading, following and walking beside each other, all at the same time. We find a sense of worthiness, a sense of safety, a sense of purpose. When we spend time advocating for one another, we start to advocate more strongly for ourselves too. We start to realise that we are worth our own positive energy – we are worthy of the love we give to others.

I can't tell you how much easier I found it to get in the car and drive, even though I was terrified, when I knew that it wasn't just me that I was doing it for. I was willing to bend the edges of my comfort zone, because I wanted it to be possible for my community as much as for myself. There is also a joy to be found in community – a release, a delight. The world feels lighter somehow, we understand a bit more about what is important, and we care a bit less about what is not. When we realise that we truly have a home in the hearts of others, that we make a difference to them and they make a difference to us, our belonging is undeniable.

Wherever you find community, whether it's through social media, your church, your neighbourhood, your work-place or your exercise class, make a real effort to nurture those connections. Know that it is in your showing up that you make space for others to do the same, that your unapolo-getic presence is a necessary part of the jigsaw puzzle.

We often worry that our differences and perceived faults are going to render us unacceptable to a community – that the way we trip over our words or forget names, or the way we sometimes get overwhelmed and blunted by panic, mean we can't possibly add value or real presence to a group of people. But the truth is, these differences are what adds value. A group made up of exactly the same people not only doesn't exist, but doesn't have any intricacy, any depth, any true and real connection.

That's not to say a community shouldn't have things in common – they almost always do – but we need to remember that it's the quirks and elements of our personalities unique to us that enrich a community, and make us a part of something beautiful.

CHAPTER 21

WHO ARE YOU?

We are not here to fit in, be well balanced, or provide an example for others. We are here to be eccentric, different, perhaps strange, perhaps merely to add to our small piece, our little clunky, chunky selves, to the great mosaic of being. As the gods intended, we are here to become more and more ourselves.

- James Hollis, *What Matters Most: Living A More Considered Life*

– There are few things more daunting than writing your online dating profile. Attempting to sum up who you are at your core, while also being interesting and humorous and peppering in any necessary details – honestly, it's the stuff of nightmares, and it's even harder if you've lost any concept of who you actually are.

This was the conundrum I faced when I finally downloaded a dating app for the first time. I couldn't get past the 'create your profile' section. No matter how I approached it, I could not find the words to write a small paragraph about myself. Beyond my name, age and location – which the app had 'helpfully' listed in advance for me – there was no witty or alluring sentence I could come up with to explain who I was or what I wanted.

How was I supposed to explain who I was, when I didn't have a clue?

Pre-agoraphobia, I'd had a pretty good sense of myself. I knew that I was somebody who loved to travel and wanted to do more of it; I knew that I loved caffeine and cigarettes and felt at my most creative during the twilight hours; I knew that I hated the summer, preferred the winter, loved long road trips and loud music. Post-agoraphobia, however, I didn't have any grasp of who I was without somehow relating it to my anxiety disorder. It was as if I'd found myself in this weird state of emotional inertia, where I certainly wasn't the same person I'd been five years ago, but hadn't evolved into anyone else either.

It seemed as if my entire personality, my likes and dislikes, my dreams, goals and preferences were all dictated by my fears and limitations. I didn't know what I wanted out of life. I didn't know what I enjoyed doing. I didn't know what I saw in the future for myself, because my focus was only ever on things I *didn't want* for myself.

When you've spent so many years organising your life around the parameters of all the things you can't do and all the things you're trying to avoid, you're left with very little in the way of an actual life. Your sense of self is inextricably tied to the 'you' who is anxious, rather than the whole you – the you who has hopes and dreams and preferences beyond the realms of your anxiety. It feels really hard to uncover that whole sense of self when it's been tucked away for so long, and you've more than likely become used to arguing against it.

But there is a person sitting right where you are, reading these words, who is patiently waiting to be acknowledged. There is an identity that isn't tied to your anxiety, that isn't coloured by what-ifs and restrictions. There is a you that is bursting with possibility, ripe with life and an urgency to live it. It's imperative that you start working to uncover that you. Start amalgamating it into your day-to-day life, rather than waiting for your anxiety to go away so that the more adventurous side of you can come out to play. Because if you don't, you'll remain in that strange limbo state – in the space between waiting for your anxiety to ease and waiting for your life to begin.

The truth is: *You are not just someone with anxiety.*

Although we started this journey together by exploring just how much anxiety is a necessary and normal part of you, a part that needs to be accepted and embraced, not avoided or denied, I also want you to understand that anxiety is only very small part of you as a whole and unique being.

You don't have to present yourself to life with a disclaimer, a caveat, a justification for why and how you are limited. Even if – and I know this can feel hard to swallow – *even if your anxiety sticks around in the same way as it always has* it is not your defining quality. You are still worthy of all of the experiences and dreams and adventures that your heart longs for.

⌐

There is a you that is bursting with possibility,
ripe with life and an urgency to live it.

⌐

You are creative, you are capable, you are bold, you are ever-expanding. Within you is a limitless pool of desire and knowledge and a yearning for connection and love; not just an inherent need for comfort and a biological aversion to fear. If you spend your days focusing on and living for the anxious you, then the anxious you is the only facet that will seem relevant. Conversely, if you spend your days focusing on and living for each part of you in tandem – the parts that long for joy and discovery and playfulness – you will, to borrow James Hollis's words, become more and more yourself. And more of yourself is exactly what this world needs. Not less. Never less.

⌐

Perhaps one of the most helpful things we can do for ourselves is to look at the time we've spent feeling anxious and afraid not as days or months or years that have robbed us of our identity, but rather as time that has shed us of all the things we no longer needed. That we haven't lost anything that wasn't ours to begin with. And now that we are here, stripped bare, maybe we can start to see what's really and truly underneath. Underneath the resistance, underneath the fear of shame, underneath the layers of unworthiness and expectation, underneath the tension, the tightness and the tendency to close off.

Who are you, underneath the fear of fear? What are your dreams? What are your values, your hopes? What would you most love to do? What parts of you have been waiting for their chance to come alive? What is it that makes all the parts of you feel alive??

These are the questions that I started to ask myself, journalling and meditating on them night after night, trying to figure out when I'd let my dreams and desires fall by the wayside in favour of an obsession with control. It was only in being confronted by that empty dating bio that I realised, perhaps there is very little I'm willing to learn about myself beyond the fact that I'm anxious. Perhaps there might be a tiny possibility that I cling to my anxiety just as much as I accuse my anxiety of clinging to me. Perhaps – and this was the biggest 'perhaps' of all – *perhaps there is more to me than all the things I believe I can't do or be.*

I saw, with startling clarity, that I'd spent so much time in an intimate relationship with my own fear and worry that I was yet to acknowledge the presence of any other attributes. And as it turns out, there were many. Once I started asking the question: *Who am I, if not someone who's anxious?* the answers began to spring forth with a ferocity that I hadn't been expecting.

For example, I actually did want to travel. I remember clearly the day that I had that realisation, because the force with which it came out of my consciousness was like a knock to the side of the head. I had genuinely believed – and fervently maintained – that I was just not someone who liked to travel anymore. *Is this an anxiety thing?* my therapist had asked, and I'd insisted, *No, it's just who I am. I'm a home-body. I'm a mum. I've done the backpacking and the bar hopping and the Lonely Planet guides and all that, and I'm just not into it. I'm happier at home with my family alongside me.*

You can imagine my surprise when it dawned on me that I very much wanted to travel – that there was so much of the world I wanted to explore it was almost a physical ache inside me. All of a sudden, I was filling my journal with the names of all the cities I longed to traverse, and even though that little voice popped up occasionally to say, "but, how would you …" and "but, what if …" and "I read once that you have to pay to use a public toilet there …", I allowed myself to entertain these plans and dreams as if it didn't matter in the slightest that I'm someone who panics. (Because as it turns out, it doesn't.)

I discovered that, alongside the me (and the you) who is anxious, there's a me who loves adventure, filled with an enthusiastic hankering to do things involving kayaks and mountain bikes and campfires, not necessarily in that order. There's a me that loves early morning birdwatching, a me who likes to strip off my clothes at nude beaches, a competitive me who, despite being spectacularly shit at most games, will still fight to the Monopoly death in order to win. There's the me who wanted to become a medita-tion teacher, the me who dreams of spending a summer in Italy, the me who loves to sing (despite being remarkably tone-deaf), and the me who would love to go live in a cabin in the woods for a year and learn to live off the land.

When I took my attention away from the me who is anxious, I saw that there was an entire catalogue of intriguingly diverse and wonderful attributes inside me; different dimensions and layers of my personality that had been gently tugging away at my consciousness, waiting for me to turn and follow those threads towards fulfilment. Of course, the anxious me still regularly came along for the ride. I became not altogether unfamiliar with navigating a panic attack while sitting in an airplane or driving to a campground; or there was that time I sobbed for thirty minutes on the way to a national park, because my heart wanted to hike but my body (and bowels) wanted to go home immediately.

What I found though, was that in those places where my anxiety and my craving for adventure and fun intersected, there actually existed a sweet spot in which I could live. And what's more, the longer I spent exploring that sweet spot, the more practised I became at understanding my anxiety from other perspectives. Slowly but surely I became less reactive, less involved in my own stories of doubt and fear.

The more I expanded on my own sense of self, the less my anxiety seemed to swamp my life.

The world has a wonderful way of unfolding itself to you when you declare yourself ready and willing to participate.

Your anxiety will more than likely (dare I say, definitely) play a role in your explorations, especially when those explorations involve the unfamiliar, the uncertain or the long-desired. But these other sides of you, these suppressed but vitally important parts of your psyche and soul, are just as hungry for your attention as your need for safety is, and they are just as worthy of nurturing.

It may not feel easy or comfortable to delve into who you are and what you want out of life, but I implore you: *do not abandon yourself for the sake of what is familiar.* Do not give up on your sense of wonder, your sense of excitement, your ability to grow and change and evolve. Do not give into the temptation to keep your body and mind comfortable, when what your heart wants is to shake things up, to explore and expand and become. The world has a wonderful way of unfolding itself to you, when you declare yourself ready and willing to participate.

CHAPTER 22

MAKING YOUR MARK

– Along with the question: 'Who am I?' invariably comes the question: 'What am I here to do?' I've always had a niggling feeling that I was here to do *something,* and I often wondered if my high levels of anxiety were in direct proportion to the frustration I felt at having not done it yet.

I think all of us feel that we are here to do something. This is the human need to connect in us, coupled with a desire to somehow say, "I was here. I existed. I left a mark." It's important to know, however, that the fact that you exist at all means that you have already left a mark. Author and poet, Brianna Wiest, puts it beautifully: *Your purpose is, first and foremost, just to be here. Your existence has shifted the world in a way that it is invisible to you. Without you, absolutely nothing would exist just as it is right now*[29].

But of course, finding a purpose that drives you, something that makes you feel alive and at home and remarkably passionate about your place here is a powerful way to enhance your relationship with yourself, and with the world around you. In saying that, I used to get thoroughly pissed off with the idea of figuring out my purpose. I was under the illusion that I was either already supposed to know what it was – and I didn't – or that my purpose had to be something I was good at, and I was terrible at most things.

And the fact that I was unbearably anxious seemed like it left me at an enormous disadvantage, because how can you possibly contribute anything meaningful or worthwhile when you can't even leave the house some days?

What I found out though, is that purpose is something that changes, it evolves along with you; it is also a marvellous dance between seeking and giving, learning and teaching.

My purpose for this last decade (and then some) has been to not only find my own way through somewhat precarious mental health, but to walk alongside my fellow travellers, and make the journey a little easier for them as much as for myself. My purpose has also been to connect to myself, to relearn that sense of unconditional love that I had for myself as a child, and to open the door for others to connect with themselves and love themselves unconditionally. Above all, my purpose has been to find a way to make anxiety feel a little less lonely and a little less overwhelming for all of us. I hope I've done that, in some way or other.

There is something – perhaps many somethings – that you are here to imprint upon the world. There is a way in which you will illuminate the dark places, adding brightness and vibrance and real, honest warmth. And contrary to popular belief, it doesn't have to be something you are good at. Just look to what calls to you, what sparks you and lights you up inside. It is enough that it makes you feel alive.

In my mentoring work, the subject of purpose often comes up. It seems to pop up in conversation of its own accord – it slips in among idle chatter and once it does, it changes everything. Faces light up. Tone of voice gets a little higher, a little more breathless and excited. Shoulders drop, chests open, cheeks soften. When someone is talking about what they most want to do – the message that they are here to share – their whole being starts to radiate.

I often find that the message we are here to share is the same one that we once most needed to hear. For me, that message was: *It is okay to be human. It is okay to be you.* Everything I've done, everything I've worked towards, every way I've tried to get to know myself and learn myself and remember myself, has been with that message at the core of it all, for me as much as anyone else. And in speaking about it out loud, I've found that this is the message that has most resonated with others too. Those words had a way of finding the people who needed them. Whether expressed through words, music, dance, art or the way you tend to those you love, your message will find its way to the people who need it too.

The challenging part, in my opinion, is in making the decision to share/express what's in your heart. That seems to be when we come up against those old neural pathways; when we allow ourselves to be led towards the comfortable and the familiar, as opposed to the uncertainty of letting our voice be heard. Especially if you've struggled with the concept of 'being seen' (as anxious folk often have) it will feel uneasy to announce yourself, to make the transition from thinking about sharing your message to actually sharing it, even with just one other person besides yourself.

We ask ourselves: *Who am I to do this? I'm not good enough or qualified enough or knowledgeable enough; I don't know the answers; I don't know what I'm really doing at all.* We let these doubts act as bricks that we build around ourselves, creating a wall between everything we are here to do and be, stopping us from acting upon it, in case we get it 'wrong'.

But I'm here to tell you: *you will not get it wrong.* The art that you are here to make, the words you are here to write, the song you are here to sing, the love that you are here to share ... that magic can only be created by you and you alone, so there is no yardstick to compare it to. The only way you can ever really get it 'wrong' is by neglecting to answer that call within you, that burning desire to finally do the thing you long to do.

The world has been ready for you since the moment you were born. It is in embracing that fact and finally allowing yourself to be seen, to be heard, to be a glittering piece in this strange and beautiful kaleidoscope in which we all live, that you will not only find home within yourself, but the world will find its home within you too.

CHAPTER 23

FALLING IN LOVE WITH YOURSELF

*Document the moments you feel most in love
with yourself – what you're wearing,
who you're around, what you're doing.
Recreate and repeat.*

- Warsan Shire, British writer and poet

- I came across this quote by Warsan Shire while scrolling Pinterest in the early hours of the morning, as one does. It stuck out at me because, while it seemed like something beautiful and worth aspiring to, the concept of 'falling in love' with myself was so foreign that I couldn't think of one moment where I might possibly feel a smidgen of affection, let alone love, towards myself.

I thought of this quote often over the next few days and weeks. It kept reverberating in my head: *Document the moments you feel most in love. Recreate. Repeat. Recreate. Repeat.*

I was intrigued by what it might feel like to really love myself. I was so used to tearing myself apart, wishing I were someone less afraid, less anxious, more 'normal'. I was so accustomed to wishing myself out of my own body and life. I'd never once stopped and thought, *I really love who I am.*

And so I started to take notice. I began to deliberately pay attention. What I found was that it wasn't that I was without love for myself, but that I was just really practised at focusing on resenting myself instead. It turned out that the moments I paid most attention to were the shitty ones, the uncomfortable ones, the moments in which I felt distressed, unsure and wrong for this world. There were moments where I felt at home and, yes, in love with myself, but I usually let those moments slip by unnoticed, because they weren't the ones that required anything from me. It felt unnatural to not need to do anything. To just be okay. Noticing pleasure, as opposed to pain, was something I was remarkably out of touch with, and that surprised me. I'd thought that pleasure wasn't there at all. I didn't realise that I'd been the one who was shutting my eyes to it.

We need to remember what it's like to feel in love with who we are, and we do this by deliberately paying attention to who that is.

I think that for many of us who deal with heightened anxiety in the long term, the concept of pleasure is one that is entirely forgotten. Pleasure is something that fails to make a blip on the radar of survival; it's not deemed important when the body is under threat. Similarly, feeling love for ourselves seems more or less inaccessible when we're constantly pushed up against thoughts, emotions and feelings that we really don't like. When anxiety is at a peak, and the pressure of trying to contain it is overwhelming – it feels impossible to imagine a moment where we might let go and enjoy ourselves.

But we need to. We need to seek out pleasure, for the same reason that we need to connect and belong and express what is within us. We need pleasure to reintroduce balance, to tip the scales back towards the things that warm us, soothe us, restore us. We need to remember what it's like to feel in love with who we are, and we do this by deliberately paying attention to who that is. What you will notice, if you slow down and really look, is that there are indeed moments when you come alive. There are tiny little slivers in your day when you are at your most genuine, when you are the truest expression of yourself. And the more you pay attention to these moments, the more you become familiar with what that true expression of you looks like, feels like, sounds like. And the more you will seek out areas where you can expand on that.

For me, those moments were ... sitting on a chair in the library, cross-legged, pen in my mouth, writing the words of my soul (the same words that you now hold in your hand). Running on the treadmill, red-faced and sweaty, stepping in time to a beat. Floating in the water – any water – ears beneath the surface, listening to the sound of my heart pulsing, echoing in the deep. Jumping on a trampoline, double-bouncing the kids, breathless with joy. Watering the plants outside, letting the hose spray over my bare feet. Making shapes on the yoga mat. Drinking a piping hot cup of tea. Turning the pages of a new book. Cooking at the stove, music playing throughout the house, a glass of something sweet and syrupy in my hand. Reading to my eldest, making the characters come to life. Looking up, remembering how big this world is, and how grateful I am to be a part of it.

Remember when we spoke about the dark places? About how panic attacks, repressed fear and extreme discomfort can cause us to feel as if we are smothered in darkness, completely hidden away from the light? And if we hang out there for too long, keeping our eyes closed tight, shutting ourselves off from love and joy and the hearts of everyone around us, we start to believe there is nothing for us here. We become convinced that we aren't worthy of existing because we are fundamentally flawed. Damaged. Disordered.

The practice of paying attention is how we begin to let the light filter through. It's how we realise that everything we were looking for is already here – we just weren't looking at it. We realise that our ability to love has not been hindered by our fear. We notice that the things we thought were gone were actually just overshadowed by doubt and worry. Now that we've let in a little more light, we can see it all clearly, maybe for the first time in years.

I urge you to start paying attention – to start seeking out and recording the moments where you feel most like yourself. Keep your list somewhere special to you and revisit it often. Add to it as many times as you can – but don't ever remove anything from it.

If you like, you may even expand it to include moments where you felt proud or excited, or moments where you opened up instead of contracting and closing away. Eventually, it will become a habit – this record-keeping of pleasure as opposed to pain – and the way you perceive yourself will start to shift. You will start to look towards yourself for comfort, for soothing and for love, instead of looking for it everywhere that it's not.

You will start to trust yourself implicitly; you will know that you are capable, that you are ready, that you are deserving. You believe in who you are, because you've remembered exactly who that is.

CHAPTER 24

WHOLE

Remember, in the vast infinity of life, all is perfect, whole and complete ... and so are you.

- Louise Hay, motivational author and speaker

– There is something about bookstores that makes me feel like I'm exactly where I'm supposed to be. I love meandering through the aisles, picking up titles that call to me. I love the colours of the books, I love the way they sit snugly alongside one another, each one heavy with the promise of wisdom that I haven't yet discovered. Whiling away an hour or more in a bookstore feels like time well spent to me.

That was where I was headed one chilly afternoon in Lake Tekapo, New Zealand. We had arrived in town just a few hours earlier. Anthony, my partner, was taking a much-needed nap in our campervan, and I was strolling along the lakeside, making a beeline for the bookstore, excited to see what new titles I would discover.

What made it more exciting though, was that I'd recently received the news that it would soon be *my* book on the bookshelves. A few weeks before we had left for New Zealand, I'd answered a call from Leon Nacson, the then Managing Director of Hay House Australia, to tell me I'd won the Hay House Writer's Workshop competition, and that they were going to publish my book.

This book.

That news had been life-changing for me. It was a dream come true. Since I was little girl, I'd imagined that I'd one day write a book that would sit in the hands of strangers, bringing them joy, comfort, happiness … or just the understanding that they aren't alone.

When I received the call from Hay House, it felt like another way in which my life was blooming. Since I had stopped fighting my anxiety, and started actively seeking out opportunity and adventure, even though oftentimes anxious and afraid, I'd stumbled my way into so many blessings that I almost couldn't believe my life was real.

Days after I'd had that realisation about being someone who *did* want to travel, I'd gone on a first date with a man I'd met through a dating app. I wasn't expecting anything exciting, just hoping to share a meal and hopefully a laugh with another human being. In fact, going on the date was part of a commitment I'd made to myself to show up to life more fully, and to meet myself more in the process.

I certainly hadn't anticipated that I would leave that date feeling as if I was walking on air, having met someone that made my stomach flip in the most delicious way. Anthony was funny, quick-witted, and objectively gorgeous, and as cliche as it sounds, he just felt like home. Suddenly, I had found myself not only a boyfriend, but someone to adventure with! We had already travelled all over Tasmania, throughout Victoria, taken road trips to Sydney and Adelaide, and New Zealand was next on our list. My heart was full. I was happy and blissfully in love.

My daughter – my beautiful, intelligent, wise-beyond-her-years daughter – had recently started school and she was thriving. She was happy, gentle, hilarious and taught me something new every single day. I'd found a job with a company I loved, working part-time and studying meditation on the side. And I didn't know it yet, but I would leave New Zealand with a new little life growing snugly in my womb. Another little girl. Our second daughter. Although the world had changed since the pandemic and everything seemed like it was still all over the place, I was grateful. For my family, for my health, for the fact that I was here, willingly taking up space among it all.

Midway through my walk to the bookstore, I stopped. Not because I panicked, but because the view over the lake was absolutely breathtaking. There is quite literally something in the water in New Zealand that results in the most spectacular turquoise colour. It's 'rock flour', also known as glacial flour. When the surrounding glaciers shift and move, they pulverise the rock on the valley floor and grind it into a fine dust, which gets sifted into the water below. The rock flour is so fine that it remains suspended on the surface of the water, resulting in a turquoise colour being reflected back when the light hits it.

I sat on a park bench beside the lake, my hands tucked into my pockets to stop them from going numb (it was a mild 3°C, after all), staring at the brilliant blue of the water. I considered how utterly strange and incredible it was to be sitting where I was. If you had told me at the height of my struggle with agoraphobia that in a matter of years, I'd be travelling around the South Island of New Zealand in a campervan with my partner – spending our days mountain biking, skiing, hiking and kayaking – I simply wouldn't have been able to fathom it. Actually, let me rephrase. I would have been able to fathom it – but only with the notion that I'd be able to do it once I'd successfully cured and eradicated my anxiety disorder.

Once I'd got rid of panic attacks, once I'd figured out how to be anxiety-free, then sure – anything was possible. Hypothetically. But if you'd told me the truth, that I'd do the trip while still occasionally experiencing panic attacks (some that would bring me to tears, some that would leave me cranky and snappy, and some that would make me so convinced of an urgent need to poo that I'd interrupt our taxi driver animatedly telling us all about his children in order to say, *Excuse me sir – exactly how long is this drive going to take?!*) then, I would not have believed you.

Because surely, it wasn't possible to have both adventure and panic at the same time. There was no way I could be that same person – the same anxious, highly-sensitive person – and go gallivanting to other countries, doing things that required me to be in a car for hours on end, or away from a toilet for an indeterminate length of time, or stuck on a questionably long chairlift on the side of a mountain, for god's sake. How could any of that be possible if I were still plagued with those same fears, those same worries, those same awful physical sensations? And more importantly, *why would I want it to be possible?* Why on earth would I want to continue to scuttle through life knowing that, at any second, a panic attack could be just around the corner, ready to pummel me into the ground, humiliating me, shaming me, robbing me of any sense of meaning or fulfilment or normalcy?

The thing was, of course, that back then I was operating under the assumption that anxiety had the power to do all of those things. I thought that being someone with anxiety meant that I couldn't also be someone with an enjoyable and meaningful life. But as it turns out, the fact that those panic attacks still occasionally come out of left field and leave me winded, and that I worry overly and care deeply and think about things just that little bit too much … what that actually means is that, to me, life is precious.

Those moments of high anxiety are often punctuated by a vast appreciation for the world around me, for the people I come into contact with, for the places I get to go to (even if I sometimes cry on the way there).

⸝

*We fight, and we flee, and we freeze, and we forget
that this is what it means to be human.*

⸝

My anxiety hasn't robbed me of my chance to have a meaningful life. If anything, it's made the meaning clearer. To live. To live courageously and speak about the things that are so often shrouded in shame, like obsessively needing the toilet, feeling unworthy and insecure, feeling unable to leave the house and fear, in all its manifestations.

My intention to step forward into my anxieties, to explore and take up space in the world even though I've felt unable to do so at times, has led me on a path that has changed my life irrevocably. It has led me towards friendships that span oceans, a love that is better than I ever dreamed of, and an insatiable hunger for knowledge about humans and our need for safety and nurturing. It's led me to a book deal with my dream publishing house, to opportunities to meet my heroes, to vulnerable and honest and eye-opening interviews with people from the other side of the globe. It's led me, quite literally, through valleys and mountaintops and rivers, up rock walls and down icy slopes, meeting myself in places I never thought I'd see.

Most valuably, however, it's led me back to myself. To inhabiting my own body and mind again, without feeling as if I needed to be better or different or cured. I realised that it wasn't that I needed to find wholeness as much as I needed to be willing to traverse it – from the very sharp edges of my comfort zone, to the flowing, wild expanses of my hopes and dreams. You see, we long to feel that we are complete, yet we are frightened of opening ourselves up to see all that 'complete' encompasses. We want to cherrypick the admirable qualities and traits – confidence, creativity, bravery – out of the messier, less comfortable ones, like shame, indecisiveness and apprehension. We want to know an extraordinary life without the prickling of fear, or the weight of uncertainty that comes along with it.

We fight, and we flee, and we freeze, and we forget that this is what it means to be human.

I want you to do something for me. As you sit here, reading this book, please just take a moment to become aware of the person that you are. Become aware of the person that you've been. Become aware of the person that you are growing into. Notice that at the core of all of these versions of you, there is a kind, compassionate heart that continues to beat. There is a soul who has held you, carried you, walked alongside you, remained steady within you. There is a body that has grown through fear, pain, heartache and worry, as well as joy, excitement, love and hope. There is a mind that has done what it was designed to do – to steer you through life in the safest way possible, avoiding risk, threat and discomfort, to the best of its ability. Learning, remembering, wiring and firing to ensure your efficient survival on this earth. Each of these components, these facets of your being, are doing the best they can at any one time.

As you sit here acknowledging this, can you take a moment to honour each of these parts of you? Can you offer a space for all of you – the anxious, the capable, the afraid, the courageous, the dark and the light – to coexist? Can you notice your heart expanding? Notice your capacity to grow, to hold space, to comfort.

It's time to come home.

It's time to realise that we are, and always have been, whole. That there was never any part of us that was broken or wrong; that every time we tried to wish away parts of our experience, we were only turning further away from ourselves.

I hope that throughout this book, you've seen that every time you were scared, every time you resisted or asked "but, what if?" in an attempt to stay safe, every time you berated and resented yourself for being a thinking, feeling, human being, you were not doing so because you're somehow damaged or chemically imbalanced.

I hope that you've learnt to acknowledge your courage as much as your fear, to turn your heart and ears towards the language of the body, to soften towards the chorus of sensation within. I hope you've learnt that it's safe to open up and connect, even if your automatic response is to contract and close off. I hope you've come to realise that your anxiety is as much a part of you as your joy, your playfulness, your desires, your fears – but that it's no more, and no less.

I hope that you collect all of those experiences that you've tried to wish away, that you gather every part of you that you've attempted to remove or repress. I hope that you realise – truly realise – that you are wildly capable, and that this life, this world, is not closed off to you because you have anxiety. Rather, that this world has just been waiting for you to realise that you have always belonged, exactly as you are.

And that you have always been here.

Courageous.

RESOURCES

Beyond Blue

24/7 support for anxiety, depression and suicide

https://www.beyondblue.org.au/ 1300 224636

Sane Forums

Mental health support forums in Australia

https://saneforums.org/

Black Dog Institute

Medical research institute dedicated to mental health

https://www.blackdoginstitute.org.au/

Lifeline Australia

Crisis Support. Suicide Prevention

https://www.lifeline.org.au/ 13 11 14

PANDA

Perinatal Anxiety and Depression Australia

https://panda.org.au/ 1300 726 306

Headspace

National Youth Mental Health Services
https://headspace.org.au/

Reachout

A safe place to chat anonymously, to get support and feel better
https://au.reachout.com/

Turning Point

Addiction treatment, education and research
https://www.turningpoint.org.au/ 1800 250 015

NAMI

National Alliance on Mental Illness
https://www.nami.org/ (US) 1-800-950-NAMI (6264)

MIND UK

Support and advice to empower anyone experiencing a mental
health problem
https://www.mind.org.uk/ (UK) 0300 123 3393

ENDNOTES

1 https://www.goodreads.com/quotes/1270568-if-you-don-t-see-the-book-you-want-on-the

2 Javaid, S.F. et al. (2023) Epidemiology of Anxiety Disorders: Global Burden and sociodemographic associations - Middle East Current Psychiatry, SpringerOpen.

3 Arnsten, Amy F.T., Murray A. Raskind, Fletcher B. Taylor, and Daniel F. Connor. "The Effects of Stress Exposure on Prefrontal Cortex: Translating Basic Research into Successful Treatments for Post-Traumatic Stress Disorder." Neurobiology of Stress 1 (2015): 89–99. https://www.sciencedirect.com/science/article/pii/S2352289514000101?via%3Dihub.

4 University College London. "No evidence that depression is caused by low serotonin levels, finds comprehensive review." ScienceDaily. ScienceDaily, 20 July 2022. <www.sciencedaily.com/releases/2022/07/220720080145.htm>.

5 Pert, Candace B. *Molecules of Emotion: Why You Feel the Way You Feel.* (1st Touchstone ed. New York, Touchstone, 1999), 206

6 Van der Kolk, Bessel. *The Body Keeps the Score: Brain, Mind and Body in the Healing of Trauma.* (London: Penguin Books, 2015), 88

7 Ruff, Michael. "Where Do You Store Your Emotions?" Candace Pert, PhD, 19 Jan. 2019, candacepert.com/articles/where-do-you-store-your-emotions/.

8 Moller, Mary .D. (2017). 2017 Neuroscience Education Institute (NEI) Congress, Presentation on the Effects of Chronic Fear on a Person's Health.

9 Brach, Tara. "Blog: The Trance of Fear." Tara Brach, 21 Jan. 2022, www.tarabrach.com/the-trance-of-fear/.

10 Not her real name.

11 Bach, Richard. *Illusions: The Adventures of a Reluctant Messiah.* (United Kingdom: Random House, 2013), 131

12 Smeets, T., et al. "Stress-induced reliance on habitual behavior is moderated by cortisol reactivity." Brain and Cognition, vol. 133, 2019, pp. 60–71, https://doi.org/10.1016/j.bandc.2018.05.005.

13 Dispenza, Dr Joe. *Becoming Supernatural: How Common People Are Doing the Uncommon.* (Carlsbad: Hay House, 2019), 29

14 Manson, Mark "Motivation: What It Is, How It Works, and Where to Find It." Mark Manson, 5 Apr. 2023, markmanson.net/motivation.

15 Howes, Lewis, director. Do This To CONTROL Your MIND TODAY (BrainWash Yourself For SUCCESS) | Joe Dispenza & Lewis Howes, The

School of Greatness Podcast, 27 Mar. 2020,
https://www.youtube.com/watch?v=RTuf7OfZ-yY.

16 Brach, Tara. "Blog: 'Something Is Wrong with Me.'" Tara Brach, 26 May 2022,
www.tarabrach.com/something-is-wrong-with-me-2/.

17 Gilbert, Elizabeth, *Big Magic: Creative Living Beyond Fear.* (London: Bloomsbury,
2015), 21

18 "Pebble Mill at One - Peace from Nervous Suffering with Dr. Claire Weekes."
(1983) YouTube, 12 Feb. 2018, https://www.youtube.com/watch?v=h8Id8tkvdzc

19 By 'self-medicate', I am not referring to regular medication taken as prescribed,
such as antidepressants.

20 Melaragno, Elissa, and Bessel Van Der Kolk. "Trauma in the Body: An
Interview with Dr. Bessel van Der Kolk." 21 Apr. 2018.

21 Mishler, Adriene. "Yoga for Stress Relief | 7 Minute Practice." YouTube, Yoga
With Adriene, 21 Dec. 2016, www.youtube.com/watch?v=qiKJRoX_2uo

22 McGonigal, Kelly. *Joy of Movement: How Exercise Helps Us Find Happiness, Hope,
Connection, and Courage.* (New York: Penguin USA, 2021), 151

23 McGonigal, Kelly. *Joy of Movement: How Exercise Helps Us Find Happiness, Hope,
Connection, and Courage.* (New York: Penguin USA, 2021), 141-142

24 Kross, Ethan, et al. "Social rejection shares somatosensory representations with
physical pain." Proceedings of the National Academy of Sciences, vol. 108,
no. 15, 2011, pp. 6270–6275,
https://www.pnas.org/doi/full/10.1073/pnas.1102693108

25 Not his real name.

26 Turner Toko-pa. 2017. *Belonging: Remembering Ourselves Home.* (Salt Spring Island,
British Columbia: Her Own Room Press), 313

27 Dougherty, Sean Thomas. *The Second O of Sorrow.* (BOA Editions, Ltd., 2018), 10

28 Allen, Ruth. *Grounded: How Contact with Nature Can Improve Our Mental and
Physical Wellbeing.* (London: Welbeck, 2020), 138-139

29 Wiest, Brianna. *The Mountain Is You: Transforming Self-Sabotage Into Self-Mastery.*
(New York: Thought Catalog Books, 2020), 168-169

ACKNOWLEGDGEMENTS

To the wonderful team at Hay House, thank you for believing in my book. Thank you for taking a chance on me. To Leon Nacson: hearing your voice at the other end of the phone telling me I had 'won the grand prize' in the writers workshop was a dream come true, quite literally. To Rhett Nacson, thank you for bringing all my cover dreams to life and for accommodating my whims on colours! And, to Rosie Barry: thank you for your endless reassurance and feedback, and your constant positivity. What a joy to get to give you a cuddle in person at Dr Joe's seminar…you are such a vibrant and beautiful human being and I feel incredibly lucky that I got to have you in my corner. And to Louise Hay, thank you for being the guiding light in some of the darkest times in my life. And thank you for the gorgeous sunsets! ("Hello, Louise!")

To Sephina Hu through KN Literary, thank you for being the first person to read my 'vomit draft', and for your guidance and insight into the hero's journey. Thank you for encouraging me to use my voice, I don't think I truly understood that I was waiting for permission to speak my truth until you pointed it out. To Melanie Dimmitt and Cassie Mendoza-Jones, thank you both for your supportive words, your faith in my ability, and your hot tips on navigating the publishing process! I'm in awe of you both and grateful to have had the opportunity to receive guidance from each of you.

To Stacey Cupo, thank you for being my unofficial editor, for always being ready with feedback, advice, and unbounded excitement. Thank you for pointing out my typos with the kind of gentle tact that is necessary for someone on their eighteenth chapter revision. You are a gem.

My heartfelt thank you to Patrick, Lucrezia and Emily for allowing me to use your words of affirmation in my book proposal, and for being the loveliest, most genuine people. Each one of you have shaped me in ways you will never know, and I am beyond grateful to be able to be apart of your lives, albeit in virtual!

To Holly, Rielee, Anna, Brittan, Lawryn, JoAnn, John, Silvia, Annie, Victoria, Belinda, Claire, Coley, Sarah, Meg, Alex, Stephanie, Kelsey, Ashley, Matt and Jess…I can't count the number of conversations I've had back and forth with you all over the years, but I do know I am blessed to have met you in the instagram world and to now hold each of you in my heart. Thank you all for allowing me to feel seen and heard and held, and I hope one day we can all hang out in person in one big anxious (and incredible) group, and marvel at how far we've all come in our own ways. It's much less lonely traveling this path in such good company. Thank you for showing me that us anxious folk have the biggest and boldest hearts.

To Bridgette, Vanessa, Em and Ali, thank you for befriending the sweaty and anxious mum who showed up at playgroup that day. Thank you for never judging me, for being secondary mums to my kids, for always having baby wipes and snacks on hand whenever I forget (which is most of the time), and for being there with a glass of wine and a shoulder to cry on when things get rough.

To my dear friends that stood by my side even though I refused to leave the house for a good while, I would truly be lost without you. Mike, Ash, Milsa, Hayles - you never made me feel ashamed or weird for even a second. You believed in me, you championed me when I couldn't do it for myself, and I treasure our friendship more than I can say. Thank you for being my people.

To my Pig, my sidekick, my bestie. Thank you for barking your way through eleven years of sock-eating, belly-rubbing joy, and for being the goodest boy going. I miss you everyday. To Chaz, thank you for being my unofficial therapy dog. Thank you for the cuddles, thank you for the endless tail wags, thank you for hardly *ever* barking at the window and for always finding a way to slip your snout into the crook of my arm when I really needed it. I hope you boys are scooting your way over that rainbow bridge.

To Courtney: thanks for being my big sis. Thank you for always being there at the other end of the phone with advice and support, and for being patient with my many excuses over the years as to why I can't do X Y or Z. Thank you for always taking a pause and a breath before reminding me that actually, I can. Thank you for looking after me, more times than I can count; especially when you dropped everything to fly interstate and parent me (and my child) for a fortnight when my life fell apart. Thank you for introducing me to so many things that have changed my life, including yin yoga, and of course, Louise Hay!

To my mum and dad, not a day goes by that I don't reflect on how lucky I am to have you as my parents. Your hard work ethic and endlessly positive attitudes are what I aspire to. I can't begin to thank you for every single thing you've done for me over the years, but I hope you know I am grateful beyond words. I will continue to FaceTime you everyday to ask useless things like 'what is this rash?', just because I really like to hear your voices and see you all the time. I love you both so very much.

To my beautiful daughters, Lila and Juliet: I will always do everything in my power to have you grow up knowing just how loved you are. Being your mum is one of the greatest gifts I've ever been given. You are miracles; both of you - you are inspiring, creative, intelligent, beautiful forces of nature. Go get 'em, girls.

And finally, to my partner Anthony, thank you for always being the voice of reason whenever I spiralled into self-doubt. Thank you for allowing me the time and resources to focus on writing (even if I did spend most of it getting distracted by Pig and Charles), and thank you for holding my hand every time I panicked on the way to one of our adventures.

I can't wait to panic on the way to Italy with you.

We hope you enjoyed this Hay House book. If you'd like to receive
our online catalog featuring additional information on Hay House
books and products, or if you'd like to find out more about the
Hay Foundation, please contact:

Hay House LLC, P.O. Box 5100, Carlsbad, CA 92018-5100
(760) 431-7695 or (800) 654-5126
www.hayhouse.com® • www.hayfoundation.org

———

Published in Australia by:
Hay House Australia Publishing Pty Ltd
18/36 Ralph St., Alexandria NSW 2015
Phone: +61 (02) 9669 4299
www.hayhouse.com.au

Published in the United Kingdom by:
Hay House UK Ltd
1st Floor Crawford Corner,
91–93 Baker Street, London W1U 6QQ
www.hayhouse.co.uk

Published in India by:
Hay House Publishers (India) Pvt Ltd
Muskaan Complex, Plot No. 3,
B-2, Vasant Kunj, New Delhi 110 070
Phone: +91 11 41761620
www.hayhouse.co.in

———

<u>Access New Knowledge.</u>
<u>Anytime. Anywhere.</u>

Learn and evolve at your own pace
with the world's leading experts.

www.hayhouseU.com